Fathers & Sons

Fathers & Sons

RICHARD MADELEY

SIMON &
SCHUSTER

London · New York · Sydney · Toronto

A CBS COMPANY

First published in Great Britain in 2008 by Simon & Schuster UK Ltd
A CBS COMPANY

Copyright © 2008 by Richard Madeley

1 3 5 7 9 10 8 6 4 2

Simon & Schuster UK Ltd
1st Floor
222 Gray's Inn Road
London WC1X 8HB

www.simonsays.co.uk

Simon & Schuster Australia
Sydney

A CIP catalogue for this book is available
from the British Library.

ISBN: 978-1-84737-083-9 (Hardback)
ISBN: 978-1-84737-084-6 (Trade paperback)

Typeset in Palatino by M Rules
Printed in the UK by
CPI Mackays, Chatham ME5 8DT

To my adored wife Judy, for her unfailing encouragement during the writing of this book, and to my beloved daughter Chloe, for not minding that I didn't write about fathers and daughters.

Not this time, anyway.

Contents

We are the children of many sires,
And every drop of blood in us
In its turn . . . betrays its ancestor.

– *Ralph Waldo Emerson*

Preface

I was twenty-one when my father died, suddenly and with no warning to anyone but himself; a few twinges in his chest which he put down to a hurried breakfast or strained muscles from a weekend spent vigorously forking the rose beds.

His last morning on earth was spent prosaically at the office. By lunchtime the symptoms of coronary thrombosis must have been unmistakable, because Dad did what many men are strangely compelled to do when their hearts give notice of imminent convulsion – he headed for home. Perhaps men instinctively seek the privacy and sanctuary of their cave when catastrophe beckons; at any rate, my father managed to drive himself to his front door, fumbled desperately with the key, staggered inside and collapsed into my appalled mother's arms.

He had three minutes to live.

Dad said that his arms and hands were tingling and he felt very cold. Mum settled him on a sofa, called an ambulance and rushed upstairs for blankets. When she got back to him, he was now struggling to breathe but, ever the journalist – a career he'd begun thirty years before – managed to gasp: 'My expenses from last week . . . they're in the glove box.'

My mother urged him to lie still and wrapped her arms around him. This was to prompt my father's last words. As is often the case with final words, my father's proved to be disappointingly mundane. No last pearl of wisdom; no sweeping but pithy summary of forty-nine years of existence. 'Do you have to lean on me so bloody hard?' he gasped, before his life winked out with the sudden totality of a power cut. The light of my mother's life had been snapped off with a querulous rebuke.

Like most sudden deaths, my father's triggered multiple impacts. My mother, still a relatively young woman in her early forties, now faced the prospect of completely rebuilding her life. My sister and I had to face up to the prospect of a future without a father's guidance and love. Even in the depths of our grief I think we all knew, deep down, that we would adjust, absorb the shattering blow, and adapt. But for one member of the family, this would be quite impossible. For this person, the death of Christopher Madeley on the afternoon of 8 August 1977 would shroud what remained of his own life in speechless sorrow. That person was my grandfather. Geoffrey Madeley, my father's father, never recovered from the loss of his youngest son – a son he never once told he loved.

*

Geoffrey, Christopher, Richard and Jack. Fathers and sons, four generations strung together like beads on the twisting double helix of their shared DNA. Utterly unalike when regarded from some angles; almost clone-like in their similarity when viewed from others. Climbers roped together through space and time, mostly barely conscious of distant twitches on the line, but sometimes pulled up sharp by a sudden unmistakable tug from the past.

The story you are about to read spans a century, from 1907 to the present day; a hundred years of unprecedented change and transformation during which British society convulsed as never before. With these paroxysms, the roles of men and women within the family were fundamentally altered. Fatherhood evolved into something very different from the models of the past.

Men now face major challenges to their traditional position in the home. The lines between motherhood and fatherhood have become blurred, and that burgeoning new science of our era – psychology – has ushered in a new age of self-awareness and analysis. Today's fathers must surely have more insight into their roles as parents than previous generations, and yet they are probably just as confused as their forefathers were.

So begins our expedition; a survey of the lives of Madeley men that may chart a map of sorts for other fathers and sons. It is a long way back, and some of the details passed down from events that took place over a century ago have been blurred not only by time but by subtly differing family accounts. I have tried to reconcile these here.

But be in no doubt: these are true stories.

We start with my grandfather, and a tale of childhood abandonment and cold-hearted exploitation that could have come straight from the pages of Dickens.

Chapter 1

———

KILN FARM

My grandfather awoke on a feather bed in a bare room that smelled of apples. His ten-year-old mind struggled to remember where he was and why he felt a growing sense of excitement. Then consciousness returned; he was in the orchard room of his uncle's and aunt's farmhouse. He, his parents and his six brothers and sisters – all of them, from baby Cyril to big brother Douglas – were halfway to Liverpool. They'd said goodbye to their old home in Worcester the day before and packed their belongings on to a horse-drawn cart. This was a place called Shawbury. Mother and Father had told them they had one more day's journey before they would see the great ship that was to carry them all across the sea. Father said they should be prepared for storms and enormous waves.

My grandfather turned to discuss this thrilling prospect with the brother he had shared the bed with, but the other was up and gone. As Granddad hurriedly dressed, he wondered why the house was so still and quiet. Everyone should be up and preparing to leave by now. They'd meant to set off at dawn, but the sunlight slanting through the window on to the brass bedstead told him that morning had broken hours ago. Why hadn't anyone thought to wake him? Surely they couldn't have forgotten him!

Not quite. As the small boy trotted and then ran from room to room, each as silent and empty as the last, the children and parents whose names he called out in increasing desperation and panic were already long gone on the road to Liverpool. My grandfather had not been forgotten.

A deal had been done.

He was left behind.

*

The whole thing was Bulford's fault. Bulford didn't mean anything by it; he didn't set out to bring down a catastrophe on my grandfather's head, a stunning blow that would judder and ripple down through generations of Madeleys to come. Bulford was simply taking care of business; in this particular case, *his* business.

'Mr Bulford, from Birmingham.' That's how this turn-of-the-century businessman was always referred to by my grandfather's side of the family. Bulford was the money-man in a partnership with my great-grandfather Henry George Madeley. Henry was a farmer's son from Shropshire but had no intention of working on the land. As soon as he could he left the farm in the care of his two bachelor brothers and spinster sister and set up shop, literally, down in Worcester. With Bulford's backing he opened a grocery shop in the city's Mealcheapen Street. Business was brisk enough for Henry to marry, sire seven children, and live comfortably with his wife Hannah at the family home half a mile away, in Stanley Road. By 1907 their progeny ranged from baby Cyril to fifteen-year-old Douglas, with my grandfather, Geoffrey, coming in at number three. Geoffrey was ten. He didn't know it, but Bulford from Birmingham was about to terminate their happy hearth and home with casual abruptness.

Bulford called Henry to a meeting. He was sorry to inform him that he had decided to retire from business, and would therefore be removing all his capital from their joint venture forthwith. He was sure Henry would do very well by himself.

Henry was stunned. He tried his best to find a new backer but there were no takers. He couldn't go it alone; his partner's sudden exit meant the end of the little shop on Mealcheapen Street and, it seemed, the Madeleys' comfortable life in genteel Worcester. Henry had seven mouths to feed – plus himself and Hannah. Cyril had arrived only months before Bulford dropped his bombshell. Henry had to come up with some-thing, fast, or his family would be out on the street.

There was always the farm . . .

Henry's brothers William and Thomas were still up in Shropshire with their sister, Sarah. She looked after the two men while they worked the tenancy on Kiln Farm. With its tiny herd of a few dairy cattle it wasn't exactly a goldmine, but maybe something could be worked out.

Kiln Farm stands close to the village of Shawbury, about

seven miles outside Shrewsbury. A century ago, it was a remote place to live. A few miles to the south rose the dark, barrow-shaped hump of a prehistoric volcano, the Wrekin. Standing like teeth along the western horizon lay the Stretton Hills, and behind them, Wales. Kiln Farm nestled in the shallow, almost saucer-like depression of the Shropshire Plain, Roman-hot in summer, arctic-cold in winter. Few places in England are as far from the sea and the region has the closest thing this country knows to a Continental climate.

Henry had absolutely no intention of returning to live there, and still less of going back to work on the land. He'd been gone much too long for that and, anyway, his brothers were unlikely to welcome an extra tenant farmer sharing their meagre profits. Besides, where would they all live? A rented tumbledown cottage out in the sticks was unthinkable after the comforts of Stanley Road.

But Henry began to think his brothers might be willing to help him in other ways. There was nothing to keep him and his family in Worcester. Come to think of it, there was nothing to keep them in England at all. Henry knew people who had emigrated to Canada and by all accounts were getting along very well there, thank you. Why shouldn't the Madeleys do the same?

For one insurmountable reason. He had no money to buy transatlantic tickets, and no money to get his family established once they had arrived. But surely a loan of some sort could be arranged? William was his brother, after all.

Henry went back to Kiln Farm. Alone. He had no collateral to offer, he explained to William, other than his word. William told him collateral would, unfortunately, be required, but not to worry.

He had a proposal of his own to make . . .

*

The farm, so strangely quiet this sunny morning, had been full of happy noise the night before. Of course, the little ones didn't really know what was going on. Cyril was still a baby and not even talking yet. Katherine, who was three, Doris, eight, and William, five, seemed to think they were off on holiday somewhere and Geoffrey could understand why – it *did* feel as if they were off on holiday, only, well, somehow much *bigger* than that. He and his two older brothers, Douglas and thirteen-year-old John, knew exactly what was happening. They were all about to emigrate. Leave for Canada, and never come back, not like you had to from a holiday.

Geoffrey went to sleep dreaming of silver dollars and snow.

A few hours later, running in increasing panic through the empty bedrooms, he realised something else in this unfolding nightmare was all wrong. Everyone's bags had gone. Everyone's but his. He rushed down the stairs to find his aunt and uncles sitting by the kitchen fire. They looked uncertainly at each other. Then Uncle William said they had something to tell him.

*

Quite who explained to my grandfather why his family had secretly abandoned him is a question with tantalisingly different answers. One family version has it that Henry took his family to Liverpool via Shrewsbury, and then delivered Geoffrey in a detour to Shawbury. If so, was the little boy informed of his fate during the short journey, or on arrival? He had holidayed at Kiln Farm the previous year – rather oddly, the only one of his brothers and sisters ever to do so – so perhaps he thought he was being taken there to say his goodbyes. This alternative account has a somewhat less emotive quality, but it seems to me even more cold-blooded than the first.

Both my parents always believed that my grandfather arrived at Kiln Farm with everyone else, and was left behind in a dawn – or perhaps even midnight – flit. I am certain he never got to say his farewells because when I was a teenager, on one of my long walks with the old man, I asked him, 'Didn't you even get a chance to say goodbye, Granddad?' and with perfect composure he replied: 'No. No, I didn't.'

So what was Henry's 'arrangement' with the eldest brother, William? No contract was ever discovered; it is probable the whole deal was done on a handshake. Some in my family know nothing of any arrangement; others – including my parents – were absolutely certain there was one, and say my grandfather spoke of it long years after.

It was certainly William who would have set the terms. And what terms! He would advance the money for one-way passages to Canada for everyone except Geoffrey. At ten years old, the boy was William's natural choice to stay behind. He would soon be strong enough to help out on the farm, and young enough to give the maximum years of service before reaching his majority.

William threw in a couple of sweeteners. When Geoffrey was twenty-one, he would be 'allowed' to visit his family in Canada. This, eleven years after they had all sailed there without him! Of course, it was up to him whether he came back to England or not, but if he did, and assuming he was up to the job, he would be promoted to farm manager. If by then William had succeeded in his ambition to buy the farm, he would leave it to Geoffrey in his will. He had no children of his own, after all. That was the offer. Henry could take it or leave it.

Henry took it. At what stage he broke the terrible news to his wife – that she was to be parted from her third-born child, that her little Geoffrey was the price her husband had paid in exchange for a fresh start in Canada – we do not know. But we do know that Hannah was distraught. Years later her youngest child, Cyril, would visit my grandfather in England and describe to him their mother's 'awful grief' at having to leave her beloved boy behind.

What wrenching, desperate exchanges husband and wife must have had in the privacy of their cabin.

They need hardly be imagined.

But still their ship pounded inexorably westwards to Quebec. Henry's decision was irrevocable.

Hannah, even in her grief and anger, must have realised that. For what was to be done? Unthinkable to spend the stake money William had advanced them on return tickets to England, there to reclaim their abandoned son. How would they pay William back? How would they live? Where would they live?

The die had been cast. Geoffrey's fate was sealed from the moment his father and uncle shook hands on their deal at Kiln Farm a hundred years ago.

Some years before he died I asked my grandfather who had given the news to him. He maintained a wonderful silence for so long that I thought I had offended him. Then finally he said, so quietly that I could barely hear: 'It was a very long time ago. They all thought they were doing their best.' But he confided in my parents that it was his Uncle William who delivered the *coup de grâce*.

At the time, Granddad later revealed, the shock of being abandoned was total. He said the panic and fear were so intense as he grasped the depths of his betrayal and sacrifice, he could scarcely breathe. Ten years later he would experience the living nightmare of trench warfare in France, but even the grotesque horrors of shelling, gassing and hand-to-hand fighting – a smooth euphemism for the worst that men can do to each other face to face – were less dreadful to him than the crushing moment when he realised he had been deserted and delivered into a kind of serfdom.

Not that he meekly accepted his fate without a fight. That night, after a day spent speechless with shock, he was put to bed by candlelight. Geoffrey waited, motionless, for the household to fall asleep. As soon as he was certain, he slipped out of bed and dressed as quietly as he could. He had formed a plan; a plan so sickeningly bold it made him dizzy with apprehension. He would slip out of the house and follow the pitch-black lane to the village. He knew the way. Once there he would knock at the first house with lights still burning and ask for directions to Liverpool. He'd start walking there straight away and, with luck, hitch a ride on a cart or wagon after daybreak. He could remember the name of the ship and he'd find it somehow and . . . well, his parents would have to take him with the others then, wouldn't they?

It was a hopeless plan. It is almost fifty-five miles from Shawbury to Liverpool and he would quickly have become lost and been picked up by the police – but he was too little and too desperate to understand that.

Or to unpick the lock on the stout wooden door at the foot of the stairs which had been thoughtfully turned with a key. A key that was, of course, no longer there.

*

It is difficult for us today to fully appreciate just how isolated and rudimentary ordinary rural life was as recently as the early decades of the twentieth century.

My grandfather's new home was a brick-built Victorian farmhouse set in fields sloping down to the River Roden, which rolled slowly towards the Severn a few miles downstream. Across the river lay the village, reached by an ancient stone bridge. There was a pub, the Fox and Hounds, which served local ale brewed in the sleepy town of Wem nearby; a village store, the church, and some cottages. That was it – a world away from the little boy's suburban upbringing in bustling Worcester.

There was no electricity or gas supply, and no mains water. One of the first tasks assigned to my grandfather was to 'pump up' first thing each morning, vigorously working the long wooden handle of the well pump behind the farmhouse. Sometimes the water refused to rise and he would have to prime the pump with a bucket of water kept by from the previous day. Then the crystal-clear, icy-cold liquid would gush from the pump's iron mouth to fill the waiting jugs and basins.

Communications were extremely poor. There was no car, no telephone and no radio. This was years before the BBC. Newspapers were more or less unavailable, unless someone walked or took a cart into Shrewsbury or Wem, and why would anyone want to do that? Labour on the farm was gruelling, with only rudimentary mechanisation; carthorses did the work of the tractors that lay many years in Kiln Farm's future. Work filled each day and bedtime was decreed by the setting of the sun, with a candle to light you to bed.

Few visitors came to the farm. Geoffrey's new guardians were unmarried and childless, so there were no playmates on hand for him there. Quite how my grandfather adjusted to the sudden disappearance of brothers and sisters from his daily home life, let alone his mother and father, I can only guess at. But today, more than a century after he was lodged like a puppy at kennels with three virtual strangers, it breaks my heart to think how lonely and betrayed he must have felt, knowing all the time that somewhere, unimaginable miles distant, his siblings were greeting each new day together, with their parents at their side. At times, he confessed much later, he thought he would never see any of them again.

But as well as his loneliness and the sense of crushing

rejection, he must have also felt thrust backwards in time. His parents were a modern, forward-looking couple, inheritors of a bright new century and with the confidence and verve to sail the Atlantic and put down new roots in the vibrant and rapidly expanding New World. Yet here he was, trapped in a rural backwater, to be brought up by three bucolic products of the Victorian Age – an age that had barely passed. When Granddad came to Kiln Farm the Queen had been dead for less than six years.

William, who by primogeniture was the unchallenged head of the household, believed in hard work and thrift, which translated into backbreaking labour and a sparsely furnished, spartan home environment. How Granddad must have yearned for the softer comforts of his old life in Stanley Road, the sound of his brothers' and sisters' laughter, and the touch of his mother's hand. The double blow to his self-esteem of first being abandoned and then having to accept that he had, in effect, been bargained away, must have been devastating. Not that he let on to anyone what his state of mind was; not then, and barely at all later. In one of his rare descriptions of the situation he confided just two succinct words to me. He had been, he said in his usual quiet tones, 'utterly miserable'.

He was not treated like a slave, or a servant. He was, after all, family, and his guardians would be answerable for his upbringing. But he had undoubtedly become something dangerously close to a chattel: a human being who had, effectively, been bought and paid for. But he was not dealt with especially harshly, by the standards of an age when children, it was generally agreed, should be seen and not heard.

His spinster aunt seems to have done her best to welcome, calm and befriend the child who had so suddenly and unexpectedly entered her life. Approaching middle age, Sarah Madeley had long ago given up hope of marriage and bearing children of her own, and now fate had delivered her a son, of sorts. Meanwhile the boy, instantaneously deprived of a mother's love and attention, reached out with both hands for a substitute.

Was Sarah consulted about Henry and William's arrangement? It seems unlikely. Even at this distance the whole thing has the authentic smack of a classic fait accompli. I doubt even the boy's mother was informed until the last possible moment, judging by her reported reaction. But we must remember how different times were then. Women were second-class citizens. They were denied the vote. Men were even allowed to beat their wives if they believed correction was necessary.

As an unmarried sister, Sarah would have had very little leverage in the affairs of her brothers, and in any case, William was his own man with a ruthless streak. If that were not already clear, his actions in years to come would put the question beyond doubt.

Sarah, I am sure, had no choice but to accept the situation concerning Geoffrey, and tried to help him adjust to his new life. She had no experience of bringing up children and had to rely on memories of her own nineteenth-century childhood. But my grandfather probably gave her a few guidelines based on the things his mother used to do for him, before she vanished from his life. Back in the never-to-be-regained world of Stanley Road, Hannah had a tradition of making rice pudding every Sunday. It was not long before Sarah was replicating the recipe, and remembering, too, to serve Geoffrey's portion complete with its 'Mary Jane' – the obscurely named skin of browned milk and sugar that always formed on the surface and which was his favourite part.

But neither of her brothers could replace Henry in Geoffrey's affections.

Meanwhile, as 1907 turned into 1908, Granddad had no option but to make the best he could of the hand his father and uncle had dealt him. He went to the church school in Shawbury, where his superior city education swiftly elevated him to the top of the class. The headmaster was a Mr Caswell, whose wife also taught there, and their darkly pretty daughter Maudie was in Granddad's class. They quickly became childhood sweethearts; Maudie was another feminine salve helping to heal Granddad's bruised heart and was probably a sister-substitute, albeit one with romantic overtones. And friendships with other boys must have gone some way to easing the burden of his loneliness.

But the greatest soothing influence, then and for the rest of his life, was music. Geoffrey had begun piano lessons in Worcester when he was six and was allowed to continue them in Shawbury. By the age of twelve he was accomplished enough to be invited to play church organ in the neighbouring hamlet of Morton Mill.

Music became my grandfather's lifeline, his salvation. When he was playing, or attending the regular classical recitals that were one of the mainstays of rural entertainment in those pre-broadcasting days, he was transported from Kiln

Farm and the dull heartache that never seemed to leave him. Long before the age of counselling and therapy, my grandfather took reassurance and comfort from Handel, Beethoven, Chopin and Strauss. And as we shall see, great music would provide the language – the only language – through which he would be able to communicate emotionally with his youngest son. My father.

*

Slowly the seasons turned, and what remained of my grandfather's childhood gradually unwound with them. Occasionally a letter would arrive from Ontario, where Henry and Hannah had settled with their six remaining children. Geoffrey must have replied to these missives but nothing survives of the correspondence. I wonder in what terms the exchanges were made? It is certain that Hannah was still desperately missing her lost boy, but what did she write of the reasons for leaving him behind? Did she apologise? Did she ask for forgiveness and understanding?

For his part he lived and breathed for the day, still long distant, when he could follow his family across the Atlantic. If my grandfather harboured any bitterness about his abandonment he never expressed it to a soul; not then, not ever. He steadfastly refused to allow resentment or anger to stand in the way of his ultimate goal – to get back to the way things had been. Expressing his anger, anguish and bitter disappointment would not help matters.

But it could not have been easy. My grandfather was

probably the most deliberately non-judgemental man I ever knew.

Meanwhile, he was growing up. He left Shawbury school and was sent to a private school in the nearby village of Astley. William paid the fees – four pounds and ten shillings a term – but not for long. A year later Granddad was deemed to be adequately educated and, more importantly, finally strong enough to begin working full-time on the farm. He was now fourteen years old.

Did William pay him? Up to a point. Of course he was 'all found' with his bed and board, and he told my mother that William allowed him one shilling a week. As Sunday was a day of rest – as far as it could be on a working farm – my grandfather was effectively earning tuppence a day; less than three pounds a year. But the money was of vital importance to him. He immediately began saving. With an iron will, he denied himself whatever small pleasures such a tiny wage might afford him, and hoarded virtually every penny away. He had a picture, which burned bright and sharp in his mind, of a day seven years in his future. He could see it clearly: the heart-stopping moment when he would walk into a Liverpool shipping office and, with his own money, buy himself a ticket. His passage to Canada.

By the time Granddad left school, Kiln Farm had seen its herd of dairy cows swell to a modest seven heads. Butter and milk were sold at the door. Mixed crops were grown and, gradually, almost unconsciously, the teenager settled into the timeless rhythm of the seasons. He discovered, slightly to his surprise, that he was – unlike his father – rather good at farming. In fact, he began to suspect that he might have something of a flair for it. He had his own private ideas on how to increase yield and productivity, although he had to be careful how he suggested them. William was a proud and prickly character who kept his thoughts to himself and preferred others to do likewise.

He was also good with figures. Arithmetic and maths had been his strong subjects at school and now he was developing a head for business. Perhaps when he eventually got to Canada he would, after all, have something to show for all his lonely years, a set of skills that would be valued there. How proud his mother and father would be of him.

Each spring, the adolescent boy would tick off another birthday on his private, inner calendar. By the time he reached sixteen, on 8 April 1913, his goal at last seemed to be, if not within reach, at least within sight. Five more years before he would be twenty-one and free of his father's and William's 'arrangement'; free to rejoin his family abroad. What a year that was going to be! It would be the happiest, he was certain, of his whole life, the point where everything would come gloriously right at last. The date seemed to glow in warm, golden numerals whenever he thought of it.

Nineteen eighteen. The final, apocalyptic year of the Great War.

Chapter 2

———

FRANCE, FAMILY AND BETRAYAL

Like most young men in 1914, my grandfather thought the outbreak of war with Germany was rather exciting. This scrap with the Kaiser had been a long time coming and it was time to get it over with. The Royal Navy and British Army were second to none. Our battleships, and an array of crack regiments battle-hardened by the wars of Empire, would swiftly carry the day. Everyone said so. The whole thing would be over by Christmas, and then things could get back to normal.

Rarely in British history has the national mood been so catastrophically at odds with impending reality. The delusion that the coming conflict would be swift, decisive and glorious pervaded every level of society. Young men – and not-so-young men – were falling over themselves to enlist, if necessary lying about their ages and medical conditions in order to fight for King and Country.

Enthusiasm to put on a uniform and pick up a gun ran

through all the social classes. The influential and well-connected writer, Rudyard Kipling, pulled every string possible to have the son he adored, Jack, accepted for military service. Jack repeatedly failed army medicals because of chronic short-sightedness, but his father would not have his son denied the chance for glory and finally succeeded in wangling a commission for him.

Jack Kipling was killed as soon as he arrived in France. It was a pitiful death. Lost and stumbling somewhere in the mud and smoke of the trenches during an assault, he simply disappeared – he was virtually blind without his thick spectacles – and Rudyard was plunged into guilt and remorse that remained with him for the rest of his life.

The causes of the Great War are argued over to the present day, but it was fundamentally about empire. As a sea-going nation Britain was deeply unsettled by the rapidly growing German Navy, and this rivalry on the high seas was the engine that helped drive the world into madness. Tensions in Europe were so high by the summer of 1914 that it only took a single shot to ignite them into open war. On 28 June a Bosnian Serb assassinated the heir to the Austro-Hungarian throne. There was immediate retaliation against Serbia and one by one a long chain of intricate alliances was activated. Declarations of war were tossed around like confetti and within weeks most European countries were at each other's throats.

Hardly anyone really understood what had just happened but the British cheered enthusiastically anyway when war broke out. At least this was a chance to show the Germans who was boss. Jingoism was nothing to be ashamed of in 1914 Britain.

Life at Shawbury was largely unaffected at first. Geoffrey was seventeen now, and reckoned the whole shooting match would be over long before he got a sniff of the action. He continued to quietly put his shillings aside, and had no doubt that 1918 would see him departing, on schedule, to Quebec.

But disquieting rumours of unexpected setbacks on what had become known as the Western Front began to filter back. Newspapers – more people in Shawbury seemed to be reading them these days – persisted with their jingoistic, upbeat tone, but word of mouth was spreading as the first wounded began to straggle home. There were mutters that the British and French armies were stalled along hundreds of miles of snaking trenches and dugouts. Huge offensives to break the deadlock were being cut to pieces by machine guns and colossal artillery barrages.

The word 'carnage' began to be whispered. It was becoming clear the only soldiers for whom this war would be over by Christmas were dead ones.

One morning, long after the harvest and as the winter wheat was being sown, a neighbour called at Kiln Farm, clutching a copy of *The Times*. The man was shaking his head in disbelief as he pointed to a seemingly endless list of British dead and missing. 'It was so long my uncles said it was obviously a mistake,' Granddad recalled. 'It must be a list of the wounded, not those killed in action, and the paper should be ashamed of all the unnecessary grief and suffering it had caused.'

There was no mistake. As 1914 dissolved darkly into 1915, Geoffrey Madeley began to realise, for the second time in his life, that events beyond his control were again shaping his destiny. But this time he would meet fate on his own terms.

One fine morning he put on his best suit, walked into Shrewsbury, and enlisted.

*

His first military shock was an entirely pleasant one. The King's shilling was payable on a daily basis, unlike William's weekly offering, and overnight Geoffrey saw his income increase sevenfold. If he came out of this war alive, he would at least be able to afford something better than steerage class to Canada. He had long been familiar with the principal shipping lines' transatlantic arrangements.

Eighteen-year-old Private Madeley spent his first night in the army at Shrewsbury Barracks, and two days later got his marching orders. Far from being packed off 'tout suite' to the slaughterhouse across the Channel, he was posted in the opposite direction, to northeast England. Cavalry was still considered to be a battlefield option and that gave my grandfather, with his experience of horses on the farm, an intermission between the harshness of his life so far and the horrors that would shortly follow.

Sixty-odd years later, when I was working as a television reporter, I filmed a story at beautiful Druridge Bay in County Durham. I mentioned it to Granddad. 'Isn't that near where you were stationed for a while during the First War?'

I can still see the look of delight that spread like sunlight across his face. 'I learned my horsemanship on those sands!'

He told me of golden hours galloping along the seven-mile beach. Service life seemed like a paid holiday. And for the first time he had the companionship and friendship of comrades. Life in the army had bonded them all tightly together. Those boys who reminded him of Douglas and John were not blood brothers, but a band of brothers nonetheless. Suddenly, life wasn't so bad.

It couldn't last. Cavalry training was abandoned when the British and Germans realised horses weren't much use against machine guns. Granddad found himself back on a troop train, this time taking him to the trenches. Stalemate on the Western Front persisted, as did the massacres. The facile optimism of three years before had evaporated and reinforcements like my grandfather knew they were headed for the most efficient killing fields the world had ever known.

His train pulled in to Crewe Station for its last stop before the embarkation points. As coal and water were taken on by the locomotive crew, men wrote final letters home to be posted at the docks; others smoked cigarettes or pipes and made attempts at gallows humour. My grandfather stared out of the window at another train that had halted at the station.

It was crammed with troops also bound for France. But there was something different about these soldiers, or at least their uniforms. Granddad suddenly realised they were Canadians, sent to help the mother country in her hour of need. He knew from a recent letter from his mother that his two older brothers had joined up back in Toronto. Could they be on board? The chances were hugely stacked against it, but still . . .

Granddad found himself shouldering his way through the packed carriage to the officers' compartment.

'Permission to speak, sir.'

'Carry on.'

'That train across there, sir . . . it's full of Canadians.'

'What of it?'

'My brothers, sir . . . they're serving in a Canadian division. I haven't seen them for – in a very long time indeed. I'd like to cut across and see if they're on board.'

The officers must surely have thought this boy was on a wild-goose chase but permission was granted anyway. Perhaps odds were called and bets made on whether he'd find either man.

Meanwhile my grandfather had doubled over to the other platform. He took a deep breath and climbed on to the Canadian train.

It was even more crowded than his own and he only had a few minutes. He began pushing down the carriages, calling their names.

'Is there a Douglas or a John Madeley on board? Does anyone know a Douglas Madeley or a John Madeley . . .'

When I went to see the Spielberg movie, *Saving Private Ryan*, I shivered at the scene where Tom Hanks pushes his way through an endless column of soldiers, calling out for a Private Ryan. I suddenly saw my grandfather as a young man forcing his way down a packed troop train in an earlier war, shouting out his brothers' names to disinterested and preoccupied soldiers.

Still he pressed on, refusing to give up hope.

He found Douglas and John sitting together in the same carriage.

I don't know how he would have recognised them. Perhaps he had been sent a recent photograph; perhaps their faces were still discernibly those of the boys who had slipped away from him in the night so many years before. Perhaps another soldier simply pointed them out.

But it was an electrifying encounter. Geoffrey was looking into the eyes of his dear brothers, faces he had not seen for ten long and lonely years. They stared back, dumbfounded, at their lost brother, who they remembered as a little boy and who was now a strapping young man of twenty in uniform. An incredible coincidence had reunited them as they were all poised to plunge into the whitest heat of war.

It must have seemed like a miracle.

Perhaps it was.

The Madeley brothers knew the chances all three would emerge unscathed from France were slim. But they would have made no mention of that. Their hurried, snatched conversation (how strange Douglas and John's Canadian accents must have sounded to Geoffrey!) ended with promises to write and, God willing, perhaps meet in France. Then my grandfather had to go. His train was leaving, and he walked back to it in a daze.

A reunion in such extraordinary, unlooked-for circumstances is unthinkable in today's world where we can all track each other's movements through multiple lines of communication – mobile phones, emails, Facebook. But ninety-odd years ago, in the wartime bustle of a railway station in the Midlands, my grandfather found his brothers thanks to a sudden dart of almost animal instinct that had whispered to him they were close at hand. I have never believed it was simply an incredible coincidence; I think he felt their presence, somehow picked up a metaphysical signal and followed it to its source.

He never saw Douglas again. The eldest Madeley boy went into action a few weeks later in the Canadian Corp's assault on Vimy Ridge. This pimple of land in the Nord Pas de Calais region was the scene of some of the fiercest fighting of the war. Douglas was killed on the first day. John also took part in the battle, but survived.

Douglas Madeley lies somewhere near Vimy Ridge. His name is carved on the Canadian war memorial there. It is all that is left of him.

*

My grandfather was a typical veteran of the Great War in that he rarely spoke about what it was like to be at the centre of the bloodiest conflict in history. Like the huge majority of men who survived the carnage, he came home and refused to talk about it. But much later, in old age, one or two stories slipped out.

One recalled a ferocious German assault barely held off by his trench, the attackers surging so close to his position that he could see every detail of their faces as they fell to his platoon's frantic rifle-fire. Afterwards, my grandfather stared in disbelief at the shreds of skin smoking and peeling from his right hand; the bolt of his Lee–Enfield .303 had become almost red-hot during the intense firing. He couldn't understand why the mechanism hadn't jammed.

Then there was the sight of a comrade, one arm cleanly shot off by a burst of machine-gun fire, running in tight circles, screaming, before collapsing in death.

One especially vivid glimpse into hell took place on a warm summer's afternoon when Granddad was sent with a message to the field hospital. When he got there he heard peculiar growling noises coming from behind a tent. Curious, he went to see what it was.

Four or five men were suspended, upside down, from meat hooks clipped to a metal A-frame. They were in the last stages of lockjaw – tetanus – and as their spines arched in the agonising death throes, medics thought some small relief could be found by inverting them.

Within days of arriving at the British trenches near Rouen, Granddad, like everyone else, was lousy. When the parasites weren't dining on their host, they would hide in the seams of the men's uniforms. The soldiers who'd been out there for a while showed the boy from Shropshire how to de-louse clothing, passing the flame of a candle smoothly along the stitching, paying special attention to the backs of collars. On cold nights nobody wanted to take off their tunic, and the men would help each other burn lice off the backs of their uniforms.

When I was about fifteen I once asked my grandfather if, as a young man barely twenty, he had been afraid of dying. Actually, I didn't. By then I had learned that direct questions about his experiences in the trenches never got a reply; one had to pose them as more thoughtful musings. I said something like: 'I expect a lot of you – especially the younger ones – would have been very shocked and afraid. One minute you were safe in England, the next you were in the lines, fighting for your lives.'

After the long pause that always followed such not-so-subtle attempts to get him to describe his experiences, he answered: 'Well, you see . . . we didn't really talk about all that. No point. I think there was a silly song at the time, "We're here because we're here because we're here." Something like that. Everyone was in the same boat and you just had to get on with things and do your best . . . knowing it was the same for everyone was a sort of help.'

And beyond this handful of stories and comments, my grandfather's war withdraws itself into a privacy. Except for this postscript. After he had told me about the men dying of tetanus, I asked another question – one too many, I think, although there was no reproach in my grandfather's eyes as he looked steadily into mine. I can clearly remember the scene: we were standing in a glade in an autumnal Epping Forest, foraging for sweet chestnuts. Finally he spoke. 'Believe me, Richard . . . that was nothing like the worst of it.'

God knows what appalling secrets my grandfather – and millions like him – kept locked inside their heads. Some literally went mad, others withdrew into an interior world for the rest of their lives. Granddad probably saw himself as a survivor. He had managed to absorb the crushing fate of being abandoned as a child, and had long ago determined his own strategy to reverse it, a strategy fully in place as he prepared to head home after the armistice in late 1918, more or less in one piece. He had lost part of one foot, from a machine-gun burst, and would be permanently deaf in one ear after a shell landed close to his trench. Both wounds were more or less hidden disabilities: his one good ear allowed him to continue to appreciate music, although years later the arrival of stereo hi-fi would be of little interest to him; the damage to his foot was mitigated by careful scissorwork to his shoes, home-made incisions in the leather that eased the pressure on his scars. He managed to walk without a limp.

But he was twenty-one and at last the master of his own destiny. He now had more than enough money to pay his own way to Canada and rejoin his family. No one and nothing could stop him.

The British Army had other ideas.

My grandfather was sent to Ireland to fight the IRA. He had absolutely no interest in joining another shooting match after somehow surviving the Western Front, and bitterly resented his new posting.

Ireland was in turmoil. After the failure of the uprising in 1916, elections two years later saw the establishment of the Dail Eireann – the first underground Irish Parliament. By the time Geoffrey's troop ship was crossing the Irish Sea, the war of independence was in full flow. It would be another two years before the Anglo-Irish Treaty recognised partition.

The reluctant soldier wanted to be in Ontario, not the Emerald Isle. Granddad chafed at the dreary routine of guard duty and patrol, and constantly badgered his superiors to find out when he would get his discharge papers. Later that same year, 1919, he was told. And with that he had to be content.

Weeks and months passed with agonising slowness, but at last the day came. It was to be a Sunday. My grandfather's final assignment for King and Country would be the weekly Church Parade. He wound on his puttees for the last time and marched with the others down the main street of the little town they garrisoned. After morning service they went as usual into the wooden hut next to the church to take tea and cakes, served by the staunchly pro-British local ladies. On this last Sunday, as Granddad said his goodbyes to the smiling women, he suddenly felt deeply uneasy. He couldn't work out what it was, but something was definitely not right.

He went outside, lit a cigarette, and tried to think. Then it came to him. All morning, he realised, ever since leaving barracks, he'd had a sense of being secretly watched. He couldn't explain it and later, as he packed his kit, handed in his rifle and ran to catch the boat train to England, he forgot all about it. He was done with the army and the army was done with him. Soon he would be travelling a lot further than France or Ireland.

My grandfather never claimed he'd had some kind of premonition that his friends would shortly be gunned down in cold blood. Later, he thought some kind of sixth sense had whispered to him that day. He believed that an IRA reconnaissance unit had probably been keeping them under surveillance as they marched to and from church, and he had been subconsciously aware of it.

A few weeks later, Church Parade was far from routine. As

Granddad's mates marched into town, they were walking towards ambush and death. The IRA had set up a machine gun in the hedge opposite the church. They waited patiently for the British to move well into range. Then they delivered their savage rebuke to the hated occupiers.

If my grandfather had spent many more days in the army, they would probably have been his last on earth.

*

Geoffrey settled his affairs in Shawbury and in September 1919, nearly eighteen months behind schedule thanks to a combination of the Kaiser and the IRA, he finally boarded a ship bound for Canada. It was a departure touched with sadness. He and his Aunt Sarah had become very close over the years. He appreciated the way she had tried to console him in the terrible months after he was left behind, and she had been a quiet but staunch ally in his determination to leave Kiln Farm and find his family again.

Sarah had been sick with anxiety while Geoffrey was serving in France. Soldiers who came back alive from the trenches were precious, almost hallowed beings and it must have grieved her greatly to see him leave again so soon. But she knew he had to go.

My grandfather's emotions can only be imagined as his ship nosed into the Western Approaches – so recently a hunting ground for German U-boats preying on Allied shipping as it neared British waters – and set course for Canada. He was, he realised, sailing across a wide ocean towards a deeply uncertain future. There had been very little communication with his parents in the years after they left. They had, of course, written to let him know that his eldest brother had been killed in France. Changes of address, too, were notified.

Such desultory correspondence was not particularly unusual in those days. But it meant my grandfather really only knew his family from fading memories, memories which were frozen in the year 1907. There had been the extraordinary encounter with Douglas and John in 1917, but this had been more of an emotional electric shock than a reunion.

It was one thing to dream rosy dreams of reconciliation and rapprochement. As the liner drew inexorably closer to the mouth of the St Lawrence River, Geoffrey realised he was about to confront a group of near-strangers.

What a strange voyage it must have been for the young man. As the days passed, how he must have rehearsed what he was going to say to them all. The last time he had addressed his mother and father, he had been a little boy, and they had spoken to him as a child. What would they make of this tall Englishman when he walked into their home? What would he make of them? If they had some kind of disagreement or falling out, would he find hot words of suppressed anger and recrimination rising, unbidden, to his lips?

He was probably the most preoccupied passenger on board.

Henry and his family had put down roots in the little town of St Thomas, close to the shores of Lake Erie and at the heart of the Great Lakes Peninsula. It could hardly have been more different from Worcester, or Shropshire, come to that. This was tobacco-growing country, surprisingly hot and humid in summer, but true to the stereotypical image of Canada in winter when thick snow blanketed the ground for months.

Granddad must have written to let them know he was coming, or perhaps sent a telegram. He would not have arrived unexpectedly. But he had, at last, arrived. A journey twelve years in the making, and thousands of miles in the travelling, was done.

A series of trains and buses brought him to St Thomas and the address his family had been living at for the last few years. He stood stock-still outside the simple frame-built house on a quiet street and stared at the front door. It represented the last remaining barrier between him and his family. The emotional weight of that moment must have been colossal. Finally he stepped forward, and knocked.

A pause. Then steps approaching from the other side; a woman's tread. The handle rattling and turning; the door swinging open.

Geoffrey looked into the eyes of a middle-aged woman.

His eyes.

Her eyes.

His mother's eyes.

She stared at him, and slowly shook her head. 'Oh . . . I'm so sorry . . . I truly am sorry . . . I never buy anything at the door.' She closed it in his face.

The last exchange of photographs across the Atlantic had obviously failed to imprint my grandfather's mature features on his mother's memory. In her mind's eye she still saw him as the little boy she had last seen twelve years earlier.

Geoffrey had sometimes wondered if he would recognise

his parents when he saw them again. It never crossed his mind that they might not recognise him.

He didn't know what to do. None of his fantasies about this moment had included this scenario. Eventually, he knocked again.

Now the woman looked annoyed. He spoke quickly, before she could send him away a second time.

'It's me, Mother. I'm your son. I'm Geoffrey.'

Slowly, Hannah saw the man standing on her doorstep as the boy she once knew. Her eyes widened and she put her hands to her mouth.

'Mother . . . are you all r –'

'Geoffrey . . . oh, *Geoffrey*!'

Her child had crossed the years, a war, and an ocean to come home to her. He had come home to her.

*

My grandfather moved in with his family that same afternoon. The coming days were utterly, blissfully happy. He was 'home'. But unlike the return of the prodigal son, this was the homecoming of a young man to the prodigal parents. Forgiveness could only flow one way – from him to them.

What mature, unbounded forgiveness it was! Henry and Hannah must have been profoundly grateful (and secretly not a little relieved) to find the boy they left behind so apparently free of anger. Geoffrey had every right to ask about what had been done to him and why, but he had not made his journey to deliver judgement or apportion blame. Long ago he had decided to try to understand his father's great dilemma of 1907. It would be pointless now to condemn Henry's solution to it; Geoffrey's betrayal could never be undone. But it could be healed.

And it was. Despite the passing of the years, the Madeleys were still a relatively young family. The death of Douglas at twenty-five on Vimy Ridge left Henry and Hannah with six children; five siblings for Geoffrey to get to know again. Baby Cyril was now twelve; Katherine was fifteen, William seventeen, Doris twenty, and John, the surviving eldest, twenty-five. They welcomed my grandfather back with open arms and open hearts. He felt reborn.

Granddad spent his first months in Canada earning dollars to go travelling. He picked up some casual labour on the tobacco farms and in local factories, and stayed with his parents and siblings. There was a lot of catching up to do, not least with his brother John about their experiences in France. But as my grandfather said many years later, there was 'no need to rush things'. By the late summer of 1920 the long-severed connection with his family was almost fully restored. He felt confident and relaxed enough to tell them that he was heading off for a while.

The harvest season had arrived. Geoffrey decided to use his farming skills to freelance his way west, working as casual labour until he reached the Rocky Mountains and the Pacific Ocean beyond. He began by fruit-picking on Ontario's farms, then crossed into Manitoba to help bring in the wheat. He did the same in the great dust bowl of Saskatchewan – Canada's Kansas – and by autumn's end he had reached Calgary in Alberta, and the foothills of the Rockies.

At some point along the way, he met The Girl.

The Girl. Of all the figures in my grandfather's past, it is she who remains the most elusive, and yet she would have a profound bearing on the rest of his life.

Who was she? My father only knew that she was the first woman his father fell in love with, that Geoffrey asked her to marry him, and that she had said 'yes'. She was around his own age, in her early twenties. A lifetime later he would tell my young mother that The Girl was the most beautiful creature he had ever set eyes on. But he would lose her as surely as he had lost his family years before – only this time, for good. Why?

Because he went back home.

Not to St Thomas.

To England. Geoffrey went back to Kiln Farm.

Chapter 3

RETURN TO KILN FARM

All the time Geoffrey was in Canada, an invisible, unbroken thread unwound away from him across three and a half thousand miles of land and sea. All the way back to Kiln Farm, and William. There, like a fisherman patiently paying out his line, the old uncle had been waiting. Now he judged the moment had come to start reeling the line back in.

Because before Geoffrey sailed for Quebec, his uncle had extracted an agreement from him. William was on the point of buying the farm from the Charleton Estate, which was being broken up. He persuaded his nephew to promise to return after a year or so, and become farm manager. This was not a bad offer for a wounded private returning from the utter chaos of total war. Nevertheless, looking back, it seems an odd, even unnecessary commitment for Geoffrey to have made. But I suppose he would have been feeling insecure about his reception in St Thomas, and had no idea if the new life in Canada would suit him.

―――――――

Now, happier than at any time in his life and deeply in love, he must have been kicking himself. Because his girlfriend had agreed to marry him on one condition – they must live in Canada. The Girl came from a large and close family. She knew that transplanting to England would, in those days, almost certainly mean she would never see her parents or brothers and sisters again. That was unthinkable. Geoffrey, of all people, could understand her feelings.

What was he to do?

We can be reasonably certain he wrote to William and explained how the land lay. Not only had the reunion with his family exceeded his brightest hopes, he was now engaged to be married. His fiancée refused to abandon her own family and uproot to Shropshire. Geoffrey himself was loath to be parted from his parents and siblings for a second time. He knew he had made a promise and if necessary he would keep his word, but . . . surely William could understand.

Whatever Geoffrey wrote in his letter, William's response was swift and calculated. Now, unlike the verbal arrangement he had made with Henry back in 1907, the ageing farmer made a commitment to my grandfather in writing. Geoffrey opened a reply from William which went a lot further than the promise of a job.

Come back now, he read, and you'll inherit the lot when I die. Every brick, field and head of cattle. It's all here, waiting for you. Just come back. And, yes – you did give me your word that you would do so.

Quite why William was so determined to bring Granddad back to Kiln Farm, I have never really understood. There must have been other candidates to run the business. I think it was a deep-rooted sense of possessiveness. For years he had virtually owned the boy, a near-chattel that he had paid good money for. So, he thought he could fly the coop, did he? Well, William would see about that.

Oddly enough, William's offer to leave Kiln Farm lock, stock and barrel to Geoffrey didn't weigh particularly heavy in my grandfather's decision to return to Shropshire. He would have come back anyway. He was, he explained to my mother years later, a man of his word. If William wouldn't release him from it, he had no choice in the matter.

Such old-fashioned morality is almost unheard of today; indeed, many would now laugh at it. But back then, the imperative was sufficiently strong for Geoffrey to do something that in our sentimental, romantic age, we would consider more or less unthinkable: he gave up the love of his life. Not that he didn't try to persuade The Girl to come with him; not that she didn't try and convince him to stay. But it was no use. Steel hawsers of convention, duty and circumstance dragged them apart.

A few weeks after receiving his uncle's letter, Geoffrey found himself on a ship headed back to England. His brokenhearted fiancée had released him from his promise; his anguished parents had said their bewildered goodbyes and, as he watched the icebergs drift past the liner as it steamed east from the mouth of the St Lawrence, he knew that, once again, William had succeeded in parting him from the ones he loved.

*

Granddad arrived back at Shawbury as a young man in his
mid-twenties. He had seen more pain, loss and heartbreak
than many experience in a lifetime. I think it was at this point
that the die was irrevocably cast. He had been repeatedly and
brutally separated from those who were dear to him. It almost
always seemed to happen just when he was feeling at his most
optimistic and hopeful about life. But what was the point in
showing people how much you loved and needed them if
they were taken away from you? What was the point in
making plans for happiness when, in reality, you had no control over their outcome?

Perhaps it was for the best that he had come back to the farm.
Land was land. Land couldn't betray you or leave you. And he
would inherit these acres one day. They would be undisputedly
his, for ever. No one could take that away from him.

So Geoffrey, in self-protection, began to shut down emotionally. It was a spontaneous, subconscious reaction to one
heartbreak too many. His soul had been bruised too often.

Whether my grandfather would have maintained this psychological defensive crouch is debatable; what is not is that life
was now preparing to kick him in the teeth with both booted
feet, as if to drive home some undecipherable lesson, or punishment. I sometimes wonder if he was being made to atone
for some dreadful sins in a past life.

*

Back at Kiln Farm Geoffrey quickly slipped into a familiar routine. Sarah was overjoyed to see him; she had greatly missed

her nephew. William was William, and got on with the business of handing over the day-to-day running of the farm.

Geoffrey increasingly felt that his adventures in Canada were taking on a dreamlike quality. Had he really been engaged to be married? The Girl wasn't answering his letters. Sometimes he found himself wondering if she had ever existed at all. Shawbury, with its unchanging familiar reality, was quietly reclaiming him from the New World and delivering him back to the Old.

To his surprise, he found he wasn't willing to fight the process. Perhaps the numbing of his emotions would turn out to be a positive, an unlooked-for anaesthetic for a bruised heart. And meanwhile there was the soothing balm of his music. He began playing piano again at local recitals, and one evening was asked to accompany a young woman with a light, pleasant voice. She was a couple of years younger than him, and pretty, with soft, dreamy eyes and a creamy complexion. Her name was Kate Edwards, although, she confided in Geoffrey, everyone called her Kitty. She lived on her parents' farm a few miles from Shawbury – close enough for the two of them to meet again.

It was a brief courtship. Geoffrey found himself engaged for a second time. He was slightly astonished, but it felt real enough and a sturdier situation than the increasingly fading scenario in Canada. Today, we would say he was going with the flow. We might also say he was marrying on the rebound.

Kate's parents were delighted. They had three daughters, part of a cursed generation of women. The slaughter of 1914–18 had decimated the young male population. Soon after the armistice, the headmistress of an English public school bluntly described the cold new reality to a subdued assembly of senior girls. She told them their chances of marriage were now one in ten. It was no exaggeration.

So when Kate Edwards became Kate Madeley, the gathered wedding guests could practically hear the collective sigh of relief from the bride's side of the little country church. Not only was she safely off the shelf, she was marrying one of the catches of the county, a young man who was well travelled, musically accomplished, only lightly scarred by war – externally, at any rate – and with excellent prospects.

He was also undeniably attractive. Geoffrey was lean and stood over six feet tall. Intelligent eyes looked out of a well-proportioned face. Perhaps there was something a little distant about those eyes, but they could also twinkle with humour. For most of the year he was lightly tanned from working outdoors, and he had large, sensitive hands. Kitty used to love to watch them as they moved smoothly and confidently over a piano keyboard.

Yet almost as soon as it had begun, the marriage ran into trouble. At this distance it is difficult to be precise about the reasons, but it seems there was tension in the farmhouse from the start. Sarah was accustomed to running the place single-handedly for the men; my grandmother Kitty's arrival transformed this simple arrangement into a knotty equation. As Geoffrey's new wife, she would have expected to assume considerable control over domestic matters, but where did that leave Sarah? Perhaps attempts were made to divide responsibilities, with Sarah attending to her brothers and Kitty to Geoffrey, but if so they were not a success. The atmosphere became charged and volatile. Kitty – spirited, feisty, with a strong sense of her own self-worth – decided she'd had enough.

One morning, after a spectacular row with her husband over some household matter, a heavily pregnant Kitty walked out. My grandfather's marriage seemed over before it had barely begun.

Kitty's journey home passed into family legend. I have an image of her as I write this now. She is striding across pastures and meadows, tearful but determined. I can see her as she clambers over stiles and fences, clutching her swollen belly, startling the cows grazing on the lush Shropshire grass. They lift their heads to stare at the young woman as she passes through them like a weeping apparition.

At last, an exhausted Kitty reaches the familiar fields of her parents' farm and sweeps into her mother's kitchen, telling her tale through heaving sobs.

'I've left him, mother! I've left him! I cannot bear it any longer . . . I have left Geoffrey and I am never going back.'

But if Kitty had expected a sympathetic welcome, she was in for a shock. Her mother heard her out, and then delivered an iron verdict to her sniffling daughter. This merciless lecture on the facts of life was, my grandmother wryly recalled, like having a bucket of cold water poured over her head. She told me the whole story one summer's evening as she and I moved a huge pile of logs from the farmyard into a barn.

Firstly, Kitty was crisply informed, there was the minor matter of her wedding vows – promises made before God.

Eighty years ago, Christian doctrine was the powerful glue that bonded society tightly together. Covenants made with the Almighty were taken with the utmost seriousness. My great-grandmother would have been appalled at her daughter's defiance before God, and perhaps even a little frightened by it. This argument stood by itself, but she had other arrows to shoot, more prosaic but just as pointed.

Kitty was pregnant. Had she forgotten that? This was the worst possible time to cast aside the protection of a husband. And even if she did insist on divorce – which was out of the question, by the way – what man would want a woman with another man's child? These were bleak enough times for women. Villages had seen whole generations of their young men virtually wiped out, and the survivors could take their pick of women desperate to find a husband.

No, Kitty was told, with a firmness bordering on the ruthless. You must go back and make your peace with Geoffrey. It's your duty – to him and to God.

So she went.

What was it about Kiln Farm? I know this is fanciful, but sometimes it seems to me that the place had a mysterious way of holding on to those who most wished to escape it, gently but implacably drawing them back against their will. Today, when I hear the Eagles song 'Hotel California', I think about Kiln Farm as the haunting final line is sung.

'You can check out any time you like – but you can never leave . . .'

Marriages displaying early cracks can be split apart by the birth of a baby. But in my grandparents' case the arrival of their first son, James, in 1924, seems to have brought them close again, for the time being at least. Theirs would always be a somewhat volatile marriage. My father once said it mirrored the seasons, sometimes sunny, sometimes icy.

Certainly Kitty now had a clearly defined role, as the first new mother Kiln Farm had seen in many years.

The focus of daily life must have shifted seismically. The dynamic had changed overnight; William's appointed heir now had an heir himself. The farmhouse had long felt a sterile place – strange, considering it was the hub of a cycle of life that revolved with its fields and cowsheds and stables. But now it had become a nursery. The place had a purpose and a point beyond mere business.

Geoffrey, staring at himself in his shaving mirror the day after his first-born had been safely delivered, must have considered the question all men do on such momentous mornings.

What sort of a father would he make?

It was a difficult one. His own father had been on another continent for much of Geoffrey's childhood and William had hardly been an ideal replacement role model. Although my grandfather was fully reconciled with Henry, theirs was a relationship between adults. He really had no examples to follow.

Oh, well. He would just have to do his best.

*

Granddad was twenty-seven when James was born. He was just shy of thirty when a second son, John, arrived. Perhaps

the vivid reality of fatherhood with two lively little boys running around the farm was reassuring; Geoffrey saw that life
could offer more than forced goodbyes and sudden partings.

John was a bright, inquisitive boy. Before he was three, he
became fascinated by the weekly ritual of paying the farm
hands their wages. The night before payday the little boy
insisted on polishing the copper pennies and silver sixpences,
shillings and florins. Only then was his father allowed to
count them out in gleaming towers on the kitchen table. To the
child, they looked like piles of treasure glinting there. One
Irish labourer, whose name has not survived the passing of
eighty years, made the same joke every week. The lad had, he
said, 'taken a shine' to him.

One gusty morning in early spring, John and James were
sent to play in the orchard that stood behind the house. As
usual, they were given strict instructions to stay clear of the
well, which lay like an unblinking dark eye in the grass
between the pump room and the trees. That well was still
there when I was a child, roughly boarded over but still a
brooding presence that both fascinated and frightened me.

On that chilly morning so long ago, it wasn't the well that
drew either boy to its dark mouth. The threat was all around
them as they played in the friendly orchard in the sunshine. It
was in the breeze whispering through the branches above
their heads. A dry, cold wind flowing down from the Welsh
hills on the horizon, summits still bleak in a winter that lingered around their old bald heads.

John had removed his coat as he ran around in the deceptive sunshine. Later, he began to shiver and complained of a

headache. He was put to bed and remained there the following day, suffering from a 'chill'. By evening he was running a high temperature and starting to breathe strangely. The village doctor was called: the Madeley's second son was diagnosed with pneumonia, and the parents were advised to prop the child up on pillows during the night to help drain fluid from John's chest.

The next day, he died.

He was four years old.

*

Child mortality was common right up to the Second World War and the increasingly widespread availability of antibiotics and mass immunisation. But John's illness was so abrupt, so casual in its easy, invisible arrival and swift, pitiless departure that my grandparents could scarcely comprehend what had happened. The shock stayed with them for the rest of their lives. Decades later, when my sister and I drove on visits to Shawbury with our parents, the last mile of the journey was always accompanied by the same solemn instructions.

'Don't talk with your mouths full. Comb your hair before coming down to breakfast. And *don't* mention John.'

My grandparents could barely speak of him. There were no photographs of him to be seen anywhere in the house; no favourite toy placed carefully on a shelf or dresser. It was almost as if he had never been.

Only once did I catch a glimpse of him. My grandmother kept an ancient bound-wooden chest in the farm's living room. The old box was full of the bric-a-brac of half a century, the not-quite detritus of a family's life.

I was fascinated by this trunk and one afternoon, when rain fell from the sky in pounding torrents, my grandmother gave me permission to rummage through it. I was about nine years old.

Once I had excavated the disappointing top layer of old women's magazines, knitting patterns and yellowing bills for obscure farm machinery, things got interesting. The barrel and lock of a rusting .410 shotgun – no stock – and a mouldering gun-cleaning kit that smelled of crushed walnuts. Clanking mole traps, all springs and chains and sharp snapping jaws. My grandmother had once set them under her lawn to catch the little beasts so she could sell their velvet skins to passing tinkers.

A medium-sized cannonball with the faded label: 'Moreton Corbett – Civil War'. And finally, right at the bottom, hidden by a faded embroidered cushion, a little glass jar with a brass top. It might have once contained perfume or face cream, but as I held it up to the rain-streamed window I could see it was filled with tiny balls of silver and gold paper; the kind of foil that used to line cigarette packets. There were dozens of them, and I poured a few out. What could they mean?

Suddenly a hand fell on my shoulder and I yelped with shock, scattering the little balls over the floor. My grandmother bent down and picked them up wordlessly, dropping them carefully back into the jar and gently screwing the lid back on. When she'd finished, she looked at me.

'They were John's,' she said simply. 'His money. He was too

little when he . . . well, he was too little to have real money, you see, so he made his own.' She gestured. 'The gold ones were pennies and the silver ones were shillings. When his father paid the men their wages, John used to pretend to do the same with these.'

The next day, helping my grandfather move sacks of grain in a store shed, I asked him with the directness of childhood: 'What happened to John, Granddad?'

He stood quite still for a few moments and then slowly sat down on one of the dusty bags. He lit a cigarette, considered it, and then he began to tell me about that March day in the orchard, two brothers running between the trees, and Death beckoning one of them as they played. When he'd finished, he said he'd stack the rest of the bags by himself. I never asked about John again.

John's death was, I believe, the psychological tipping point for my grandfather. Since he was ten years old he had done his best to deal with the worst fate and circumstances could do to him. He had been determined, tenacious and, on occasion, magnificently, heroically, non-judgemental. A tough self-reliance had seen him through tests and challenges that would have brought other men to their knees.

But this . . . this was too much. This wasn't fair. Yet again, someone he loved had been snatched from him. Would this be the way of it to the end of his days? Loving and losing, loving and losing, over and over again? It could not be borne; there must be some way to protect oneself from endless passages of such savage pain.

Geoffrey had wondered what sort of a father he would

make. After John's death, my grandfather quietly withdrew into an emotional fortress. The drawbridge was drawn up. Life would go on, but Geoffrey would not have his heart broken again. For the time being, he had placed it beyond reach.

Chapter 4

COLD COMFORT FARM

John died when my father was still a baby. Just over a year earlier, on 2 May 1928, the village midwife delivered the Madeleys' third son in the front room of a crooked half-timbered cottage next to Shawbury's church. The village and countryside around it had barely changed from the day Geoffrey arrived there, twenty-one years before.

It was still a quiet rural backwater. A few more families owned cars but many did not. In Shawbury, the age of the horse had still not passed.

By no means all farms and cottages had electricity, and oil lamps and candles could still be seen glowing at windows after dark. Something of the nineteenth century lingered about the place.

But appearances were deceptive. Christopher Holt Madeley arrived in a world trembling on the brink of enormous change. The signs of imminent and dramatic acceleration into an almost unimaginably altered state were there to see, if you looked for them.

In 1928, America issued its first television licences, and radio stations began transmitting pictures along with sound. Meanwhile ordinary US citizens had discovered the stock market and were making paper fortunes.

The month after my father was born, Amelia Earhart became the first woman to fly across the Atlantic. By September Alexander Fleming had stumbled upon penicillin. Mass entertainment was revolutionised with the arrival of talkies – even Mickey Mouse muscled in on the act with *Steamboat Willie* – and at a place called Berchtesgaden in the Bavarian mountains, Adolf Hitler was busy dictating the second volume of *Mein Kampf* to Rudolf Hess. Tectonic plates of social change were straining against each other. Something had to give.

It did. A few months later, Wall Street crashed.

*

By the time Christopher was four, the Great Depression had the world by the throat and Kiln Farm teetered on the brink of fore-closure. Money was so tight that all luxuries and fripperies – not that these had ever featured particularly prominently – were eliminated. But one small weekly treat for my father survived. Denied sweets or pocket money, he nevertheless received, every Sunday, a small chocolate-covered biscuit wrapped in silver paper. His mother bought it on Saturdays at the village shop and it stood in solitary splendour on the kitchen dresser until after lunch the next day, when it was solemnly handed to the little boy.

My father loved these biscuits, but after a while felt that supply was simply not keeping up with demand. He decided that with a little sacrifice, foresight and patience, he could improve matters considerably. He had watched his mother picking fruits from her orchard, and sowing seeds in her vegetable garden. Why not plant a chocolate-biscuit tree?

That Sunday he heroically denied himself his treat and took it to a quiet corner of the orchard. He scraped a small hole and crumbled the biscuit into it. Earth was brushed back over the top, and my father retired to await developments.

Every morning he ran to see if the first shoots were pushing up; each day brought disappointment. By the following Sunday he was torn: should he eat his next biscuit or plant it again? After lunch, he decided to ask his mother for advice.

Dad later told me that the reaction his innocent enquiry provoked was the first great shock of his life. Not his mother's response – Kitty listened carefully to her son's dilemma and then dissolved into helpless laughter. But Geoffrey, sitting in an armchair behind his Sunday paper, began to tremble with rage.

He rose and took a cane from a cupboard. Face dark with anger, he accused his son of 'wicked waste' and drew him into the parlour for a measured beating. The punishment lasted for at least a minute and my father would say it was at this precise point in his life that any nascent desire to sow crops was comprehensively extinguished.

It was the first time Geoffrey had thrashed his youngest son, and it would not be the last. The beatings continued until that delicate moment of balance was reached: the point where a boy realises he has grown powerful enough to consider the merits of striking back.

The dark gods of corporal punishment are complex and mysterious. It is tempting to assume that Geoffrey's extraordinarily violent response to a tiny infraction had its roots in his own childhood. There must have been a great deal of buried anger in him. He had worked so hard to rationalise everyone's behaviour and forgive it; and there had to have been a price to pay for that. Certainly my father thought so. Although like many men of his generation Dad shied away from over-analysing anyone's behaviour – including his own – he knew cause and effect when he saw it.

As he grew older and learned more about his father's fractured journey to manhood, my father was able, to some extent, to forgive Geoffrey's dramatic swings from emotional froideur to hot-blooded rage. If he concluded that his father was unconsciously lashing out against his own childhood experiences, he kept that to himself. But I think this was probably at the heart of it. And I have supporting evidence; the domino effect of these beatings clicked and tripped its painful way into my own childhood.

But these almost ritualised punishments – the sacred stick broadcasting its mute warning from corner or cupboard; the appointed place of execution (always the parlour where the best furniture was) – were not peculiar to Kiln Farm. They were de rigueur for the day. Most parents still imposed discipline on their children according to the Victorian mantra of 'spare the rod and spoil the child'. Fathers – and mothers too – cheerfully wielded straps, canes, belts, rulers and shoes on their erring sons and daughters and would have been astounded to be told they were child-abusers.

But there were limits, even in 1930s rural England, a line across which overenthusiastic child-beaters stepped at their peril. A story, still whispered years later, concerned two small children, brother and sister, who went to the same village school as my father. Pale, pinched, often badly cut and bruised, it was obvious they were being seriously knocked about at home.

One morning they appeared in class after an absence of several days. The marks on them were so severe that the headmistress brought them into her office for gentle questioning. It gradually emerged that both parents had recently been particularly free with their fists, feet and sundry objects that came to hand. The girl had compression fractures and her brother was passing blood in his urine. Both were half-starved; they had been locked in a coal shed for a day and a night.

The outcome was swift and decisive. Social services not being quite the über-force they are today, a discreet meeting was arranged that afternoon between village elders. The broken children were sent to stay at a friendly home for a few days, and that evening a small party of villagers (my grandfather always refused to say whether or not he was among them) paid a private visit to the parents. Matters were simply and efficiently laid out, a few judicious strokes of someone's walking stick were added for clarity and emphasis, and the pair were then introduced to the delights of their own coalhole.

They were released the following night, with a final reminder of their parental responsibilities. The children were returned home; the abuse abruptly ceased. Not for the first time, Shawbury – like other communities across the country – had quietly, efficiently, and of course entirely illegally, resolved their own problems.

Against this background, the beatings my father suffered were perfectly acceptable. The social norm would slowly change, and over the next thirty years such thrashings came to be increasingly regarded as grotesque.

Geoffrey's explosive reaction to a wasted biscuit should, in fairness, be placed in the context of the Depression. Every penny had to be squeezed. He was under ferocious financial pressure; neighbouring farms were going to the wall and Kiln Farm could be next. He had built his herd up to fifty head of cows with an impressive daily milk yield but local dairies were going under too and frequently there was no one to collect the brimming churns. Granddad would wait as long as he could and then, in defeat, pour hundreds of gallons of perfectly good milk straight down the drains. My father and his older brother stood with the farm hands, watching in silence as the creamy white torrent frothed and gurgled away. It was heartbreaking.

The freshly milked cows would plod back into the fields, with no one certain that the whole soul-destroying process wouldn't be repeated the next day.

Granddad kept his nerve, but on other farms in Shropshire there were suicides.

Meanwhile, it wasn't a bad place for a boy to grow up. However bad the slump got, there was always food on the table – it was a farm, after all – with eggs and cream, bacon, home-baked bread and, occasionally, a freshly plucked chicken. (I can remember as a child the days before battery farming when chicken was an expensive delicacy. On Sundays my grandmother would go to the hen coop, select that day's lunch, and wring its unfortunate neck. Back in the kitchen she'd pluck it and burn off the stubble with a lit newspaper. I can smell the sharp fumes now – a pungent odour of singed hair and burned toast.)

Sometimes the family would dine on duck. Kitty once kept a small flock as an experiment, but it was short-lived. My grandmother had a schizophrenic attitude to animals: ruthless, yet sentimental. One hot summer day she decided to lead her quacking charges down to the river 'for a little swim'. The flotilla disappeared around the first bend. Kitty's anguished cries – 'Duckies! Come back!' – could be heard in the village. The creatures were never seen again, except perhaps by foxes.

The Depression forced Geoffrey to postpone plans to buy Kiln Farm's first tractor, so huge horses still hauled the ploughs and harrows and seed machines. This was a job my father loved to help with, and he struck up a great friendship with the biggest beast of the lot, a magnificent black-maned giant called Captain.

Captain was devoted to my father. At the end of the working day he would whinny loudly for him from his stable and only settle down after the boy had come to say goodnight. Once he escaped from a carelessly locked stable door and trotted up to the drawing-room window. Christopher was practising his scales on his father's highly prized baby grand (bought second-hand before the Depression and one of Kiln Farm's few luxuries). There was a crunch and tinkling of glass, and he looked up to see Captain's great head pushing into the room like the figurehead on the prow of a ship, nostrils flared, teeth bared, lips curled back in a sloppy, happy grin of greeting.

Other animals were less friendly. When Christopher was about four years old, he went to pet Rex, the farm dog. It was a hot day and the big black Labrador was sleeping in his kennel (there was no question of dogs being allowed in the house). Rex was startled when the little boy's hand suddenly materialised through the doorway. He flew out and clamped his jaws on my father's face.

There was pandemonium as farm hands rushed to pull the dog off. When they managed to free my father, the damage looked bad. He was bleeding from both eyes and screaming that he couldn't see.

The village doctor quickly established that it was simply blood that had temporarily blinded the child, and dressed and disinfected the deep bites around my father's eyes. But the attack left lasting damage to his sight. Almost as soon as the wounds had healed, he complained of headaches and not being able to 'see proper'. An optician in Shrewsbury diagnosed astigmatism. It seems likely that the bites had disturbed the shape of the surface of both eyes, and my father had to wear glasses for the rest of his days.

So life on the farm was nothing if not eventful. But as my father grew up he often struggled to be happy. He had the companionship of James, of course, but his brother was four years older and had his own interests and circle of friends. He also seemed to have, my father thought, an easier and more open relationship with their father. Indeed James, a talented farmer, was destined to run Kiln Farm in years to come.

Like many siblings with a significant age difference, the relationship between Chris and Jim, as they called each other, would only become truly close when both were grown-up.

Christopher loved his parents and assumed they loved him, but as he got older it was hard to be sure. There was a near-total absence of demonstrative affection. Kitty was more outgoing than her husband in this regard, but not by much. My father told me he always felt his relationship with his mother was characterised by formality. My grandmother was a formidable woman with a short temper, and I think he was secretly a little afraid of her.

But Kitty was an earth mother compared with what, by now, was Geoffrey's almost complete emotional withdrawal. As a small boy, my father gradually became aware that his friends' fathers were different from his own. He would see them ruffling their sons' hair, swinging them in the air, playing games with them, tickling them, even kissing them – but nothing remotely like that had ever happened to him. It confused him. Once he was playing at a friend's house when the boy's father returned from a short business trip. His son rushed out into the lane – 'daddy-daddy-daddy!' – to be swept up in a bear hug.

My father walked home thoughtfully, and made a plan.

A short time later, Geoffrey had to spend a night or two on business in Shrewsbury. On the evening of his return his youngest son waited patiently by the wooden garden gate that opened into the lane. He was going to welcome his father home just like his friend had his.

It was almost dark when the tall figure finally emerged from the gathering dusk, smartly suited and wearing his best trilby.

My father took a deep breath and ran down the road towards him, shouting and waving. But when father and son reached each other, a terrible awkwardness descended. After a few moments, the little boy resolutely stepped forward and hugged his father's knees. There was absolutely no response. Finally he let go and stared down, utterly defeated, at Geoffrey's shiny town shoes. There was a long moment. Perhaps my grandfather felt chastened by the sight of the forlorn child before him, because he suddenly knelt down and put one arm stiffly around his son's shoulder for a brief moment. Then he stood up and walked on.

That was it. The first and last occasion in my father's child-hood when his father made the slightest gesture of physical affection towards him. Dad never forgot it. Until the day he died he could remember every detail of the moment: the 'pink-ing' of the blackbirds roosting in the dim hedgerow, the evening star beginning to shimmer in the darkening sky, the smell of his father's tobacco pouch, the colour of the tie he wore.

It was blue, by the way.

When my father first told me this story I felt almost guilty. I was around nine or ten and I felt guilty because it was clear to me – and to him – that my own relationship with my grandfa-ther was much better than my father's had been.

Granddad and I were pals, mates. He did what endears any adult to a child: he took an interest in me. He also treated me as an equal. He taught me how to play draughts and sometimes I would beat him. He didn't mind.

We swapped jokes. One Christmas Eve he insisted that the stockings my sister and I had just hung above the hearth at Kiln

Farm (we always went to Kiln Farm for Christmas) were too small, and lent us his own huge, knee-length, woollen farmer's socks instead (this became a tradition). Next morning I woke at dawn and looked out of the bedroom window to see my grand-dad, hurricane lamp in hand, walking out of a straw-filled outbuilding where some calves were kept. I thought he looked like a genial Joseph by the stable.

I loved him and always looked forward to our visits to Shawbury. My grandmother was perhaps a little distant with me in my earlier years; she doted on my sister, probably because Kitty had never had a daughter. But when I stopped being an irritating little boy (she didn't call me Richard: I was always 'Wretched') Kitty and I grew close, too.

I think my father took vicarious pleasure from all this. I also believe I was a kind of surrogate son for Geoffrey, in the narrow sense that he could demonstrate the affection to me that had been locked away inside him for all those years. When he ruf-fled my hair or kissed me in greeting or farewell, he was also doing it, belatedly, to my father.

Even so, they never managed any more than a handshake.

But it must have been hard for my dad, on the days when his father took me down to the river to fish, or told me stories on long walks through the fields. He'd never had anything like that when he was a child.

There can be no doubt that we children, and our cousins, James's son and daughter, helped to defrost the atmosphere at Kiln Farm. I remember happy family parties there, my father and grandfather laughing delightedly together, or falling into a deep discussion about their shared love of classical music.

What a terrible shame it took so long. Back in the 1930s, my father had to grow up on Cold Comfort Farm.

But if Geoffrey was unable to demonstrate love, he was nevertheless a good provider for his family. By the mid-1930s he had steered his farm through the worst of the Depression. The atmosphere at Kiln Farm became more optimistic and, perhaps best of all, he and Kitty had the place to themselves and their children. At some point Sarah and her brothers had moved to a cottage of their own nearby, to give the growing family more room. My grandmother was mistress of her own house at last.

Up to a point.

Sarah still kept a protective, almost maternal eye on Geoffrey and she made regular return visits to Kiln Farm to check that Kitty wasn't frittering away her husband's money. Before each arrival, my grandmother moved any new furniture out of sight and replaced it with the old pieces. New vases vanished from tables, rugs were rolled up. Even the newly installed telephone was hidden in the big chest in the living room, after explicit instructions to the local exchange not to connect any calls until further notice.

I don't know why the young couple was so worried about Sarah's disapproval of their modest domestic improvements. Perhaps Granddad, so fond of the woman who had done her best to be a mother to him, simply didn't want to hurt her feelings or make her feel inadequate, as if she had failed to furnish the farm properly. Or it could have been that this was no time to rock any boats, as the day of his promised inheritance drew near.

Because William was now an old man, and in failing health.

He still took a close interest in the business, but appeared satisfied with his nephew's running of the farm.

So he should have been. By 1936 Geoffrey had continued to build up his herd of prime dairy cattle. Profits were good. Meanwhile, after the fiasco with the ducks, Kitty concentrated on her hens, cultivating the orchard, and bringing up her two boys. The Madeley acres had never been so productive; Geoffrey thought that William must be proud of what he was achieving.

He couldn't have been more wrong. Just a week after his last meeting with William, the old uncle died, not unexpectedly.

The will was read.

William hadn't left Geoffrey a thing.

*

My grandfather was dizzy with shock. What had he done to deserve this second great betrayal in his life? There had been no argument with his uncle, no rift. They had last spoken the week before the old man died and Geoffrey racked his brains to remember if there had been some hint of the catastrophe that was about to explode in his face. He could think of none.

He faced ruin. All those years of grinding labour – for nothing. A brave new life and a great love in Canada rejected – for nothing. His word of honour put above the yearning of his heart – for nothing. It was a catastrophe with no meaning. Not since he was ten years old had Geoffrey felt so confused and cast aside. He could make no sense of it at all.

The shock waves from William's bombshell would ripple

through space and time – down the years into family legend, but first across the Atlantic to Canada.

Yes, Canada, once again inextricably bound up in a stunning reversal of fortune for my grandfather.

Because William had not left Kiln Farm to his sister. That would have almost certainly undermined his extraordinary decision to disinherit Geoffrey; Sarah would probably have made the farm over to her nephew or at the very least left it to him in her own will.

No, there was a surer way to put Kiln Farm beyond Geoffrey's reach.

Cleverly, thoughtfully, and with a kind of wicked capriciousness, the will divided Kiln Farm into equal parts. And bequeathed them to each of Geoffrey's siblings in Canada.

'Every field, every brick, will be yours. Only come back . . . you gave your word.'

William's treachery was grotesque. The circle of betrayal which began in 1907 now closed neatly around his nephew like a noose. In his confusion, Geoffrey could only wildly think that his success in running the farm had made his uncle jealous. I think my grandfather was wrong. Jealousy, which may well have been a factor, scarcely seems reason alone to account for an act that fell little short of sadistic.

More than seventy years later, I am convinced that William's perfidy sprang out of a terrible obsession with control. As I have said, I don't think he ever really ceased regarding my grandfather as his personal possession, a pawn on the chessboard he could move at his pleasure or sacrifice at his whim. The jealousy Geoffrey dimly discerned was, I think, something far more sinister: the tip of a monstrous hidden iceberg of malice.

William would have known full well the effect of the reading of the will on my grandfather. To be disinherited would be a heavy enough blow, but to learn that everything was to be divided amongst his brothers and sisters, who had only been in a position to go to Canada with their parents because of Geoffrey . . . this was the devastating sucker punch.

Perhaps the old uncle thought it all an excellent joke. But beyond a warped sense of humour lay, I think, a rather neat calculation. Leaving Kiln Farm to my grandfather would have been a poor endgame for William; it would be a final, irrevocable transfer of control from him to his chattel. And William just couldn't do it. He just couldn't bear to release the boy from his power.

So he did the next best thing. He transferred it to others.

Long ago, Henry had handed his son into his brother's keeping. William became the boy's guardian – legally, at least. Morally, he developed into something infinitely colder and darker.

By the end, William was Geoffrey's bane.

*

The first thing Sarah did when she heard the news was to hire a lawyer. The will had to be challenged, she said. It was monstrous. Right was right, and her brother had done a dreadful thing. Granddad wasn't hopeful, and the lawyer swiftly confirmed that the will was legally watertight. Now the focus switched to Canada. Everything depended on decisions taken there. Would Geoffrey's siblings grab their windfall with both hands, sell up and cash in their assets?

Geoffrey looked west, and waited.

Opinion about what to do was divided amongst the Madeleys in Canada, but their discussions were held in camera and it is impossible now to piece together exactly how they unfolded. All the main players are long dead, and confused stories have been passed down the years. However, it seems pretty clear that Geoffrey's fate hung in the balance. Apparently some siblings wanted to sell their share of Kiln Farm at once; others were acutely conscious of the moral dilemma with which they had been presented.

This latter group pointed out that the prosperous farm they had been jointly bequeathed was only a going concern because of their brother's sacrifice and hard work.

The opposing forces countered that Uncle William's last will and testament should be respected. Legally the place was now theirs, and they had their own growing families to consider. Geoffrey could stay on as manager; there was no question of throwing him off the farm . . .

The debate wrangled on.

According to my parents, it was Geoffrey's youngest sister, Katherine, who banged heads together at a crisis meeting held to resolve things once and for all. Legend has it she summoned her siblings to the capital of the Canadian midwest for what became known as 'The Winnipeg Summit'. Katherine, who had been barely three when she was separated from her brother, arranged the meeting at a hotel in the dusty prairie town. Once they were all there, she read them the riot act.

There was to be no more talk of anyone selling off their parcel of Kiln Farm on the open market. She would never speak again to anyone who did such a thing. They were entitled to their inheritances, but only up to a point, and certainly not at the price of their brother's happiness and security. They owed him everything.

In the end, Katherine prevailed. Back in England, Sarah paid for a lawyer to draw up contracts allowing Geoffrey to buy back Kiln Farm from his brothers and sisters. It was, Granddad would later generously say, 'an amicable settlement'. Under its terms, he took ownership of Kiln Farm in 1937 although the deeds were, for some reason, retained by Sarah. They were finally passed to him on her death fourteen years later, in 1951. Geoffrey was fifty-four years old. A long time to wait.

I have often wondered how he managed to regard the 'buy back' agreement with such apparent equanimity. I suppose it was the best offer on the table; William had seen to that. But my grandfather's acceptance of a great injustice was rooted in more than pragmatism. He had forgiven his parents for abandoning him; now he forgave his siblings for presenting him with a bill for what was rightfully his.

Why? Because I think my grandfather had grasped one of the most fundamental truths of human experience: the extraordinary healing power of forgiveness. Geoffrey had been sundered from his family once; he had no intention of allowing it to happen a second time. So he made the necessary sacrifices and accommodations.

Perhaps at the expense of relationships closer to home.

*

Geoffrey, Kitty, James and Christopher huddled round their wireless set one Sunday morning in September 1939 and listened to Chamberlain's weary voice telling them they were at war. It seemed a strangely remote prospect; after all, Shawbury had been a long way from the guns of the Great War.

The village didn't know it, but things were going to be very different this time.

Kitty wasn't greatly disturbed by the prime minister's announcement, although she thought the poor man sounded very tired. He had worked so hard to avoid this; she felt sorry for him. But she knew her eldest son couldn't be called up for at least a couple of years, and Christopher four years after that. Her husband was already too old at forty-two. The Madeley men should be safe this time and, anyway, the thing was bound to be over soon. France had a huge army and we had a navy. There was an RAF aerodrome at Shawbury now and Kitty had been summoned outside by her sons to see the new fighter planes being put through their paces high in the skies above the Shropshire Plain. Everyone said our Hurricanes and Spitfires were better than anything Hitler had.

Geoffrey was less sanguine. He had done battle with the Germans face to face and knew they were depressingly good at it, both at long range and at close quarters. They'd almost won last time; if it hadn't been for our secret weapon – tanks – they probably would have. For nearly four years their armies had been within an ace of breaking through to the Channel ports. What if they made it this time?

But to begin with, it seemed Kitty's optimism was justified. For months, nothing much happened. Perhaps Hitler's bluff had been called. Some people said an honourable truce should be announced and everyone could just go home.

May arrived. Dad woke one morning to hear his father coming back into the house from the dawn milking. There were the usual start-of-the-day noises – the fireplace being raked out from the night before; pots and pans banging on the kitchen range. Suddenly everything went quiet. Then, his father's voice bellowing from the foot of the stairs: 'Come down, everyone, now! It's on the wireless! It's started!'

German soldiers had swept into the Low Countries at dawn. The fight was on.

The phoney war hadn't just ended; it was being blasted into oblivion by events which followed each other with dizzying speed. Within a few weeks Belgium had capitulated, France had fallen and the British were fighting a desperate rearguard action in the Pas de Calais so its army could escape across the Channel. Dunkirk was a catastrophe and a deliverance. But with most of its battered army's equipment left behind, many wondered if Britain would fare any better than France if Germany invaded.

My grandfather and his neighbours working other farms in Shropshire and in the Welsh Marches met in secret soon after the fall of France. This was before the formation of the LDV – the Local Defence Volunteers, which would later become the Home Guard – and most of these men had served on the Western Front a quarter of a century before. They had a fair idea of what living in enemy-occupied territory would be like.

Late one night my father, just twelve years old, eavesdropped on one of the meetings, which were always held in the kitchen. He hid behind the door that opened on to the back staircase leading to the maid's room. What he heard astounded him. Far from the confident predictions of ultimate British victory they usually made to their families, the men were gravely pessimistic. None of them believed it would be more than a few weeks before Germany invaded. They reckoned British forces would fight bravely, but be swiftly crushed.

The occupation that followed would be brutal and murderous.

There must be a resistance movement – and they would organise the regional arm of it. They would have to make do with their shotguns, hunting rifles and the occasional revolver smuggled back from France twenty-odd years ago, but attacks on German patrols and outposts would quickly yield deadlier weapons.

My father never forgot the next part of the discussion. One farmer was saying that they would probably have to hole up in the Welsh hills. What would happen to their families? Could they manage? And what if the Germans discovered the men's identities? There would be terrible reprisals on their wives and children, without doubt. Perhaps it would be best . . . that is to say, kindest, considering these terrible possibilities . . . to . . . well . . . before they left for the hills, to . . .

The silence that followed seeped into my father's hiding place like a cold fog. His heart pounded and he could hardly breathe. Finally another voice spoke.

'If you mean what I think you mean, I'm out. What the hell would we be fighting for if we did that?'

'All right, Ted, all right, keep your hair on. But we must talk

about these things, we must think it all the way through . . .
Look, let's just forget that part for now.'

Later, the men gone and Kiln Farm asleep, my father crept to
his bedroom. To his horror he found he could see the brutal
logic in the suggestion. If these unthinkable things came to pass
and he, his brother and his mother were arrested by the
Germans, it would go very badly for them. My father was fully
aware of the Nazis' readiness to use extreme measures. Looked
at like that, maybe it would be kinder to . . . get it all over
beforehand; what people called being cruel to be kind.

But he couldn't possibly discuss it with his father; he'd be
furious at being spied on. He couldn't tell his mother for the
same reason. She probably wouldn't believe him anyway. He
himself could hardly credit what he had just heard.

In the end he made a compromise with himself. If the
Germans invaded and looked like winning, my father would
tell Kitty everything. Otherwise he would keep quiet. It was all
he could think of. And with that, he rolled over and fell into a
sleep interrupted by terrible dreams.

*

The Germans didn't invade but they visited Shawbury nevertheless. By the time Christopher entered his teens, the Blitz had
begun. Manchester and Liverpool lay roughly sixty miles north,
and the village was almost directly under the Luftwaffe
bombers' flight path. The air raids went on night after night,
and people would go outside to listen to the great flying
armadas rumbling their way to their targets. The planes were

invisible in the dark, but it was possible to distinguish between enemy aircraft and the British night fighters trying to bring them down. The German planes' twin engines weren't synchronised and gave a strange, uneven drone which I can still hear my father imitating for me when I was a boy; a sort of low-frequency ululation – sinister and unnerving.

So was the noise of bombs pulverising the big industrial cities to the north. The sound of the bombing rarely carried as far as Shawbury but the vibrations did. My father always knew when the attacks had started because the heavy balls on his brass bedstead would start to judder and jangle in sympathy with the colossal explosions more than fifty miles away. As the attacks developed and peaked, ornaments would tremble, candles flickered strangely and windows rattled as in a gale.

One winter night in 1942, the Madeleys were having their evening meal. Liverpool was that night's target and the bombing had begun earlier than usual. The familiar vibrations had been making the house tremble for about an hour when they were overlaid by something else – the drone of an approaching plane. The steady rise and fall of its engines marked it as a German bomber.

Conversation came to an abrupt halt and everyone lifted their eyes to the ceiling.

'What the devil does he want here?'

Kitty stared at her husband. 'Perhaps the aerodrome, Geoffrey?'

'Maybe. He'll have a job finding it – it's cloudy and there isn't a moon.'

By now the plane had throttled back its engines and dropped

down closer to the village. It began circling patiently, flying round and round as it sought its target. In several homes nearby, there was something close to panic and many ran to their cellars and shelters, but my father noticed that my grandfather showed no emotion other than curiosity. 'It made me realise how cool he must have been under fire in the trenches,' he said.

As the plane continued to circle, the tension on the ground became almost unbearable. My grandfather, still staring at the ceiling, said: 'His navigator must be trying to work out where the airfield is by dead reckoning. He can't possibly see it in the blackout.'

At last the pilot seemed to give up. His engine revs increased and the plane began to fly away to the south, its mournful droning gradually fading.

'Thank God,' my grandmother said, 'he's leaving.'

'Or lining up for his bombing run,' came her husband's reply.

He was right. The engine noise suddenly increased again. This time there was no tentative circling – the plane was coming in fast and low.

'Everyone to the arches!'

These were a row of thick red-brick arches set low in a kind of demi-cellar at the back of the house. I have no idea what they were originally for but that night they would have to make shift as tiny one-man air-raid shelters.

Within seconds the first bomb began to fall with a tearing, rushing sound. There was an enormous crash somewhere near and then the sound of another bomb, which seemed to be falling through the air even closer than the first. It landed barely a hundred yards to the southwest in the field next to the farm. The explosion shook the entire building to its foundations and the crouching family felt the percussive wave punch through them, squeezing their ribcages and jerking involuntary 'Ahhhs!' from them as their lungs compressed. Another bomb exploded further away, the plane roared back up into the sky and the attack was over.

The Luftwaffe pilot missed the RAF base, but his stick of bombs had neatly bracketed Kiln Farm. There was no damage to anyone or anything and, once this had been established, Shawbury was rather proud of itself. My father said it was one of the most exciting nights of his life and my grandfather was always happy to tell the tale, complete with full sound effects.

The crater caused by the closest bomb is still there but not as apparent as when I was a child. Now, the crudeness of the original scar is softened by grass and patches of nettles, always the sign of disturbed ground. I suppose the pockmark lingered so long because the field wasn't ploughed, but left for grazing. I used to make my grandfather take me to it and insist he go over every thrilling detail of that night. Once I told him I wished I'd been there when it happened. He gave me a long look.

'How odd to want to be blown up . . .'

The bombing of Kiln Farm marked the end of the first major chapter of my father's life. A new phase was about to begin.

His father was going to drop a bombshell of his own.

Chapter 5

————

EXILE

By the time he was fifteen, Chris, as he now preferred to be called, had given up any hope of forging closeness with his father. If his relationship with Kitty had been characterised by cool formality – something which was slowly thawing as he got older – that with Geoffrey remained deep in permafrost. There was simply no reaching the man and Chris had stopped trying.

There were points of contact, however. The two shared a passion for classical music. My grandfather had an extensive collection of 78s – scratchy recordings of some of the world's best orchestras and opera singers. He retired into the parlour most evenings to listen to them and Chris would often creep in and join him.

These were moments when father and son were closest. There was no need for conversation; the dialogue was provided by the great composers. I believe this shared passion for music was the invisible umbilical cord connecting the two of them, and despite all that had happened, and all that lay ahead, it was an essential link which somehow prevented them drifting completely apart. James was a part of this connectivity too; he had a fine singing voice and was in much demand at local recitals. After the war, he even made a few records.

Chris and his father enjoyed discussing politics and the course of the war, which had been going atrociously. After the fall of France, the British suffered setback after setback. General Rommel's Afrika Korps had all but destroyed our army in North Africa; the Japanese had seized Singapore after British forces barely fired a shot in resistance; at sea, German U-boats seemed poised to win the Battle of the Atlantic after sinking a colossal tonnage of Allied shipping. In Russia, it looked like nothing could stop Hitler's giant war machine and the fall of Moscow looked imminent.

Few would admit it aloud but by 1942 it appeared extremely likely that the German/Japanese axis was going to win the war. The chief of the British High Command, Field Marshal Lord Alanbrooke, wrote as much in his private diaries (parts of which were not made public until the next century).

But America's entry after Pearl Harbor would change everything. Not at first; it took a while for the 'sleeping dragon', as one member of the Japanese High Command described America, to shake itself fully awake and bring its latent strength to bear upon the enemy. But my father's abiding anxiety about the local resistance movement's putative scorched-earth policy began to lessen as it became clear that Germany would not invade. By 1943 the tide had turned; shipping losses were down, North Africa was retaken, and the Russians launched sweeping counter-attacks against the Wehrmacht. Now the talk was of a different invasion – that of Nazi-occupied Europe by the Allies.

Throughout these changing fortunes of war, Chris had been educated at Wem Grammar School, an establishment in a quintessential small country town. By 1943 he was in the fifth form and was enjoying himself there. He'd started going out with girls, to the cinema in Shrewsbury mostly, and had a relaxed approach to the looming School Certificate exams and his studies in general. He began staying out for longer and coming home later. One of Geoffrey's farmer friends saw the lad smoking a Woodbine in the Fox and Hounds, his arm around a girl.

His parents decided he was going off the rails. Something had to be done.

I have never really been able to get to the bottom of this nonsense. My father was merely going through adolescence, and as far as I can tell it was not an especially bumpy passage. He didn't get into any kind of trouble. He hadn't come to the attention of the local police. He wasn't under threat of being kicked out of Wem Grammar. Years ago I found Dad's school report for that year – 1943 – and it was entirely unremarkable. Christopher Madeley was 'a bright boy with a tendency to laziness'. He must work harder and spend more time on his homework. He could be 'a little over-exuberant in class'. If he settled down to his studies, his exam results should be 'more than acceptable' by the following term.

Big deal. Rebel without a cause Dad wasn't.

The axe fell one evening during the school holidays.

Geoffrey and Kitty had been to see a local clergyman to discuss their 'wayward' youngest. The man, it turned out, had connections with a minor public school known for its old-fashioned approach to discipline. It was miles distant, tucked away in a remote corner of rural Staffordshire.

Would the reverend find their boy a place there?

At first the man was uneasy. He told them that, at fifteen, their son would find it extremely difficult to adapt to the rigours of life in an English public school. Most boys at such establishments had been sent away from home when they were quite small, to prep schools. They had become accustomed to long separations from their families and knew how to navigate the closed, claustrophobic, arcane world of a boarding school. By contrast, Christopher would be completely out of his depth and, worse, a Johnny-come-lately. An outsider. Boys could be very . . . inconsiderate to outsiders. Even some of the staff may be, well, somewhat dismissive. These were more or less closed communities. Perhaps it would be best to leave him where he was. The reverend couldn't quite see what the problem was, but felt sure things would settle down. Besides, Wem was a good school.

But my grandparents were determined. So letters were sent, fees negotiated, and before the end of the holidays, the business was settled. There merely remained the minor matter of informing the boy concerned.

Geoffrey called my father into the drawing room.

'We're sending you to Denstone.'

'What's Denstone? I'm sorry, Father, I don't understand.'

'It's a boarding school in Staffordshire. About fifty miles from here.'

'But . . . but I go to Wem. What's wrong with that?'

'Nothing. It's you there's something wrong with. You're becoming a slacker. Denstone will put a stop to that.'

'But . . . I don't want to go away, Father. And I'm not a slacker. I want to stay here, with, with . . . everyone. I shall be terribly unhappy, I know I shall. I swear I'll work harder at Wem. Please don't send me away, please . . . surely Mother doesn't agree with this?'

'She thinks it's a very good idea.'

'I won't go. You can't make me.'

Geoffrey smiled faintly, and left the room. His son burst into hot tears of anger, frustration and sheer disbelief.

My father often described to me the day he left Shawbury for Denstone. It was the following Sunday. He and his mother took the bus into Shrewsbury, Christopher with a brown suitcase resting on his lap. All his other things would follow on in a trunk. As they neared the station he implored Kitty to change her mind.

'I still don't understand what I'm supposed to have done wrong, Mother. Please, please, please, don't do this to me. I'll do anything you and Father want; I'll ask for extra homework . . . I'll study all day on Saturdays . . . I won't go to the cinema during term . . .'

'Come on, Dad,' I asked him. 'There must have been more to it than you're telling me. Surely they gave you at least one good reason?'

No, he said, they hadn't. Not then, and not after. All he could discern was an implacable determination to send him away, a determination he sensed stemmed chiefly from his father.

So why did his parents do it? Why send him into exile; sever him from Kiln Farm, Shawbury, and all his friends and familiars? It was an extraordinary decision and he never understood it.

He never forgave them for it, either, although he managed to pretend to, much later.

Today, I believe he was right to think his father was the chief architect of the whole thing. Geoffrey is the key to understanding such an apparently inexplicable event. Fathers can be jealous of their sons and I wonder if Geoffrey was finding it increasingly difficult to reconcile his own childhood privations with my father's growing freedoms and pleasures. My grandfather was in no way a cruel man, at least not intentionally, but perhaps Chris's relatively freewheeling lifestyle (by the standards of Geoffrey's own corralled adolescence) piqued him. Dad had already announced that he had no intention of becoming a farmer (unlike his brother) and was already talking about a career in journalism; perhaps even becoming a writer.

I am sure Geoffrey persuaded himself that he was banishing Christopher to a better place for his own good, but I don't believe that was his underlying, subconscious motive. Indeed, it's possible that at a deeper level he was re-enacting his own childhood abandonment, but in mirror image. Instead of the boy being left behind, he was sent away; the long-ago sin against the father visited on the son.

After the bus had arrived at Shrewsbury Station, Kitty waited on the eastbound platform with her boy for the Stoke train. By now my bewildered father had abandoned his pleading and stood, utterly dejected and in complete silence, beside her. He simply could not understand what was happening. It made no sense to him at all.

At last his train arrived and he climbed very slowly into the carriage and turned round to look at his mother through the open door.

Kitty banged it shut with a crisp: 'Goodbye dear. See you at the end of term.' And with that she walked back through the barriers and out of sight.

My father was not a lachrymose man. In my entire life I only saw him weep once: the day John F. Kennedy was assassinated.

But I wasn't with him that Sunday on his solitary journey to Denstone.

*

After several stops and changes, Christopher found himself on an obscure branch line that delivered him to tiny Rocester Station. Denstone was just outside the village, perched on a low hill.

As my father hiked his case up the lane that led to his new home, he wondered what the place would look like. Perhaps it was an archetypal English public school; soft mellowed stone or warm red-brick; ivy-cloaked cloisters, mullioned windows and ancient elms lining the Doctor's Walk . . .

Slightly comforted by his imagination, he rounded a corner and was confronted with reality.

Denstone was a Gothic construction, a forbidding central block with twin wings on either side. My father once took me there and, even accounting for the prejudice I brought with me after hearing his stories about the place, I thought it looked more like a Victorian lunatic asylum or prison than a school. Just as he had told me on the way there, the overall effect of its frontage made it appear as if the building grinned at those who approached it. It was not a friendly grin.

But perhaps buildings absorb the atmosphere and mood of those within them. Today Denstone is a modern and popular co-ed college; the echoes of Tom Brown's Schooldays have long gone. When I went back more recently to stare at it again, the sardonic grimace of welcome had disappeared. Just an ordinary, orderly arrangement of stone and glass. It was most strange. As if the place had been exorcised.

But on that darkening evening more than sixty years ago, Denstone was as grim a destination as anyone could have wished. My father was greeted formally by the matron and informed he was one of the first to arrive for the autumn term. Hadn't his parents told him classes didn't start for several more days? Most of the staff wouldn't arrive until the following day and the boys the day after that. Meanwhile he would have to manage with bread and margarine for his supper and see himself to bed. Sheets and pillows were still down in the laundry so he'd have to make do with blankets. He could have his pick of the dormitories tonight; allocations would be made later.

And with that the fifteen-year-old boy was left with half a candle, a sliver of soap and a basin of cold water for the morning.

*

By now the war pervaded every corner of British society, and that included remote Denstone. The demand on manpower was remorseless, with campaigns under way in North Africa, Italy, the Atlantic and the Far East. Conscription had reached record levels. Those previously deemed too old, too unfit, or too important in civilian jobs, were now efficiently sucked into the voracious military machine. By the time my father arrived at Denstone the planned invasion of Europe was barely ten months away and even more men who had never thought they would see action were getting their call-up papers.

So Denstone was now staffed almost exclusively by elderly retirees. Pedagogues long ago put out to grass now found themselves back in the classroom to plug the gaps left by younger ones gone to war. These were teachers who had been the backbone of the late-Victorian age of education, and many had not taught for more than twenty years.

As my father watched these relics from another era assemble in the Great Hall in their mothballed gowns and mortar boards, he thought they looked like a flock of ancient crows. One, picking over his luggage like carrion, opened a long leather box and took out a cane. He swished it with surprising vigour through the air, nodded as if satisfied, and placed it carefully back.

Hell, thought Chris. I've come to bloody Dotheboy's Hall.

Almost everything the clergyman back in Shawbury had cautioned his parents about turned out to be depressingly accurate. My father spoke with a distinct 'country' accent. This was quickly picked up on by the other boys as they began returning from holiday and they immediately dubbed him 'our country cousin'.

Most of them had been together as a unit for years; some had been at the same prep schools. Dad was a classic outsider. Unfortunately Kitty had bought him school trousers in the wrong shade of grey; it was too late to do anything about it now and in Denstone's isolated and enclosed world such trivialities assumed tribal significance.

There were the usual induction ceremonies, more normally associated with the arrival of younger boys. Dad presented an opportunity for one last hurrah before such japes became beneath everyone's dignity. Most nights he would find his bed drenched in water; his clothes were stolen while he slept and stuffed in the nearest cistern.

But Dad was a grammar-school boy and he knew the ropes. He'd been expecting this, and adopted a stoical attitude. They weren't bad boys at heart and after a while the ragging began to flag. But it came to an unexpectedly abrupt end after someone went too far.

A special school assembly had been called to celebrate an Allied victory and the boys were instructed to make sure their trousers were meticulously pressed for the occasion. They used an old army trick. Trousers were folded with great care at bedtime and placed under the hard mattress. Done properly, the creases should be ruler-straight by morning.

That night someone gently eased Chris's trousers from their makeshift press, rolled them into a ball, and put them back.

He arrived at the ceremony looking as if he'd slept in a hedge and was instantly removed for his first thrashing at

Denstone. The maximum six strokes, too. There was disobedience, and then there was unpatriotic disobedience. Men were dying for their country and the new boy had shown gross disrespect.

There was an uncomfortable silence in the dormitory that night when my father walked in. He removed his glasses, placed them carefully on his bed and turned round.

'Who did it?'

After a pause one of the older boys stood up.

'I did, country cousin. So what of it?'

'So I fight you.'

My father was an unknown quantity to the others where fighting was concerned. They sat up in their beds with interest. Someone went to the door to keep watch.

'Come on then . . .'

Chris wasn't especially known for fighting at Wem, but he'd never lost an encounter. Since he was small, he had watched his father's farmhands settle their differences with their fists and one of them, a Dubliner called Jacob, had given him a little tuition and advice.

'Don't go worryin' about style, sorr. Just go on in loik a haymaker in a hurricane an' ye'll be foin. Watch now . . . loik this . . .'

Now, farmyard met Queensberry. Thirty seconds later, Queensberry was on the floor looking as crumpled as my father's trousers had that morning.

There were astonished murmurs around the room as my father attempted to disguise his trembling limbs by climbing into bed and pretending to read a book.

'Bloody *hell!*'

'Christ . . . are you all right, Tommy?'

'I . . . I think so . . .'

'I say, country cous– I mean, Madeley . . . well done.'

'Yes, hats off. No more nonsense, then.'

But this small victory, and the space it won him, was cold comfort to my father. He had no interest whatsoever in public school life and traditions. If he was mocked for the way he spoke, he in turn thought the way most of the other boys expressed themselves was absurd, a throwback to another age. Phrases such as 'my hat', 'good egg', and 'bad form, old boy' left him feeling more isolated than ever. He did form a couple of semi-friendships but realised the only thing he and these boys had in common was a hatred of Denstone.

And as his first term there crept into winter with agonising slowness, he had plenty of time to reflect on the fact that he had three more years of this to come. Three years, stuck in this place! Everything about it was awful. It was freezing cold, and the food was terrible – terrible. Rationing was biting hard and Denstone had no access to the occasional illicit comforts of the black market. He'd thought his first supper of bread and margarine was a stopgap before normal supplies resumed, but it turned out to be the norm. It was invariably the boys' last meal of the day, accompanied by the weakest of stewed tea with no milk or sugar. Once another boy looked up from a newspaper interview with a repatriated RAF pilot and said, 'Christ almighty, the damned POWs behind the wire are eating better than us!'

If it was an exaggeration, it was a small one.

My father began to lose weight and wrote home requesting food parcels. Suddenly his status as a farmer's son became gilt-edged. Butter, eggs, cream, cake and preserved meats arriving from Shawbury on a regular basis made Chris Madeley everyone's new best friend. But he wasn't much of a one for bought popularity and shared things out without favour.

He began to suffer from chronic loneliness.

When my father died, I was just old enough to handle probate and most of the other sad business connected with his passing. Naturally I had to go through his personal papers. One sultry afternoon in mid-August 1977, a few days before the funeral, I turned to a pile of faded letters. Most were inconsequential, but one, still in its envelope, caught my eye. It was addressed in my father's handwriting to: 'Mrs G Madeley, Kiln Farm, Shawbury, Salop' and marked 'Private'.

Denstone, Staffs.
December – 1943

Kiln Farm
Shawbury.

Dearest Mother,

I cannot tell you how much I look forward to coming home for Christmas. It seems so long since I was at Shawbury and I cannot wait to see you all again. Please tell Teddy Stiles [a friend of my father's in the village] that I will certainly be over to see him and his people before 'the big day'.

Mother, I have tried so very hard not to write this letter

but after three months spent here at Denstone I simply feel I must.

Mother, I truly loathe it here. The other boys are nothing at all like me or my friends at Shawbury or Wem and I miss them so much. I am so lonely here and the teachers are awful. Remember old Mr—— who the School Board insisted retire because he was so doddery? Well, Mother, they are all just like that here.

I do not feel I am getting the education you and father are paying for, and Wem Grammar is so much less costly for you. Please let me stay home after Christmas and go back there.

There are other matters here which I do not like but cannot explain to you.

Will you talk to Father for me?

I am so miserable here.

Looking forward to seeing you all in a week or two,

Your loving son, Christopher.

The 'other matters' my father obliquely referred to in his letter concerned a small clique of older boys – mostly sixth-formers but a few from his own year too – who preyed on smaller boys for sexual gratification. Christopher had seen nothing like this during his school career so far and it shocked him profoundly. His classmates, who had grown up with this sort of thing, advised him to ignore it but he couldn't. He had a naturally protective streak in him and was determined to intervene, even if that meant going it alone.

One day he was in the washrooms and heard sounds of distress coming from a cubicle. Two seniors were in there with a much younger boy. They hadn't bothered to lock the door.

My father dragged the two sixth-formers out but before he could do anything else they ran off. The junior scurried away too.

So that was that. It had almost been too easy.

It was. That evening, on his way to prep, the clique's ringleaders appeared out of the shadows, dragged my father into a classroom, and beat him to the floor. He was given a thorough kicking and by the time they fled he was barely conscious. He was left with temporary tinnitus and something else that until then he thought would have been impossible: an even deeper loathing for Denstone.

Christopher tried to discuss his letter with her when he came home, but she repeatedly changed the subject. A conversation with Geoffrey about it was obviously out of the question. It made for a tense, strained Christmas at Shawbury and, with a corrosive mix of frustration, resentment and anger boiling inside him, Christopher was put on the train back to Denstone in January 1944. He felt powerless, unloved, and completely rejected.

Dad never directly discussed with me the damage done to him by his parents' strange, ruthless decision to send him away. I was, of course, too young. He kept such conversations for my mother, and after he died she told me how massively destabilised he had been by what he saw as his parents' betrayal. It shook his confidence in himself, left his self-worth at rock bottom, and took him years to recover from.

The sheer, unremitting bleakness of life at Denstone left its mark too. He was, as his parents had been explicitly warned, at precisely the worst point in his childhood to be packed off and isolated in a place like that. It was simply too late. He was fifteen, not far off manhood. He had already tasted the modest freedoms of adolescence. He had no experience of curfews, compulsory lights out at bedtime, or being routinely 'gated' – barred from even going for a stroll to the village shops. Canings were frequent – far more so than at Wem – and he hated the sterile all-male world he had been banished to. Girls had been summarily cut out of his life, just as he was discovering them.

Dad never tried to pretend to me that he was happy there, but as I was growing up he used the experience as a highly selective reference library for bedtime stories. These were mostly upbeat and exciting. Such as the time a sixth-former, a loner with only one passion – Denstone's cadet force – tried to blow up the school. Everyone had gathered in the Great Hall to watch a play. Just before it began a prefect heard strange noises coming from under the stage. He and another boy pulled away a side panel and there, under the boards, was the crank, surrounded by explosives from the school armoury and fiddling with detonators.

'He was quite mad, poor chap,' my father always rounded off this particular tale. 'But after he'd been dragged away a few of us agreed he had something of a point.'

My father, as an adult, always went to great lengths to avoid discussing Denstone with his parents. My sister and I were explicitly ordered never to bring the subject up during visits to our grandparents. It was almost as taboo as mentioning John. But this keep-the-peace tactic eventually backfired; in the absence of any reproof on the matter my grandparents gradually persuaded themselves that they had done a wonderful thing for their youngest boy.

'Of course, Chris loved Denstone,' my grandmother would announce comfortably over Sunday lunch at the farm. 'It was the making of him, I always like to think. You were so grateful we got you in there, weren't you, darling? You really should think of sending Richard there, you know.'

My father, beet-red, would make anguished noises in his throat and my mother would smoothly change the subject.

He had inherited his father's capacity for pragmatic forgiveness. Although I don't think that, deep down, he ever truly pardoned his parents for causing him such pointless unhappiness, he tried his best to pretend to. Perhaps that was enough.

The Denstone years crawled by and Christopher's childhood was almost at an end. There can be no question that it had been a boyhood doubly blighted, first by his father's implacable emotional withdrawal and then by this inexplicable exile to purgatory, a sentence with no appeal.

I don't think Dad quite realised it yet, but he was now damaged goods.

I do not blame my grandfather for this, and I know my father didn't. Geoffrey had done his best to cope with the injustices and betrayals that beset him. He had provided for his family and remained strong and dignified, when many other men might have turned to the bottle, or sunk into a lifetime's self-pity. But Geoffrey had been left too damaged, too exhausted, to stop the contamination seeping into Christopher's life.

Chris was now in the upper sixth at Denstone and impatiently nearing the end of his three years there. He had increasingly taken refuge in literature and music and begun dabbling at writing. A few local newspapers had accepted letters and articles from him, mostly reviews of local concerts or reports on college sporting fixtures. Meanwhile his status as prefect brought with it slightly more privileges and freedoms, and there had been the comfort of friendships with one or two like-minded boys.

The war was coming to its exhausted end. Kitty had been right about one thing; the conflict would be over before my father was old enough to be called up, and his older brother was in a reserved occupation. Farmers were crucial to the war effort.

One peril she had remained blissfully unaware of had passed too. All of them were now safe from the tender mercies of the English resistance. Would those Shropshire farmers really have shot their own families before taking to the hills to wage guerrilla war on the occupying Germans? It seems inconceivable, yet things looked bleak enough in 1940 for it to be seriously discussed. My father never spoke to his father about that chilling conversation he'd overheard while hiding on the back stairs.

Dad carried his suitcase out of Denstone's gates for the last time in the summer of 1945. By a long-held agreement with himself, he made a point of not looking back.

Chapter 6

OVER THERE

Christopher's final school report arrived in the same post as his call-up papers.

He didn't give a damn about Denstone's last verdict on him. He had not the slightest interest in what the school thought about anything, let alone him, any more than Denstone cared what he made of it.

But he did care passionately about what was inside the brown government envelope.

My father had set his heart on joining the RAF. He'd spent hours lying on his back in Shawbury's fields watching British aircraft twisting in the skies above the farm. The damage done to his eyes by the farm dog all those years before meant he couldn't hope to be a pilot, but he dearly wanted to be part of the so-called junior service, unencumbered as it was by the centuries of tradition which dominated and stifled the army and navy.

In a rare moment of empathy, Geoffrey offered to open the letter from the War Office.

'Thanks, Dad. Go on, then . . .'

His father read it carefully, then peered over his glasses at his son.

'It's the Royal Flying Corps for you, Christopher.'

My father burst out laughing and pumped his father's hand. They grinned at each other for a moment, then looked away, embarrassed.

Many young men dreaded doing National Service. The delights and freedoms of civilian life were snatched away from them by a pitiless military fist and overnight they found themselves in coarse uniforms, sleeping in draughty huts and being shouted at by foul-mouthed sergeants. Two years of drudgery in dreary peacetime postings awaited. For some boys it was their first time away from home and many silent tears were shed during the first nights in barracks.

Not by my father. He thought he'd gone on holiday. Twenty-four months compulsory service in the RAF was a doddle after his three years at Denstone. The rigidity of service life which frustrated and oppressed so many others seemed like a relaxed and benevolent regime compared to the dark tunnel from which he had just emerged.

Luckily he was in Signals, which meant he was on the inside loop of camp life. He and his fellow telegraphists received and transmitted all official messages and requests from the aerodrome radio shack. They knew everything that was going on, from the size of the monthly potato order to the imminent arrival of the thunderous new jet fighters that were beginning to take over from old propeller-driven warhorses like Spitfires and Typhoons. Dad enjoyed being in the know before most other people. It was the nascent journalist in him. Working in Signals sharpened his appetite for exclusive information. He liked being the one to pass it on, too, and his thoughts on what he might do after his discharge began to crystallise.

By happy coincidence he was posted to Shawbury, and enthusiastically picked up the threads of his old life there, including spending as much time at Kiln Farm as duties permitted. Like his father before him, he saw no point in berating his parents for their failures. The subject of Denstone was avoided, by tacit agreement. What was done was done. Nothing could change the past. My father looked ahead now. He had a plan.

He was going to be a reporter.

During an earlier posting to Leighton Buzzard in Hertfordshire, he had talked the local paper's editor into accepting occasional articles from him, similar to the ones he'd written at Denstone. When he was off-duty, Chris reviewed amateur dramatics and concerts. After a while the editor let him cover the odd breaking story, and he took to news reporting like a natural. He had found his calling.

My father came out of the RAF in 1948, bought a stuttering, evil-smoking Norton motorbike for five pounds, and joined the *Whitchurch Herald* as a cub reporter. The paper covered a huge news area, but not much happened in this empty corner of Shropshire. Someone in the newsroom had pinned a poem by A. E. Housman to the notice board:

> Clunton and Clunbury,
> Clungunford and Clun,
> Are the quietest places
> Under the sun.

with the added scrawled line: 'Just one murder. That's all we ask.'

A year later, bored of writing up weddings, obituaries and agricultural shows, he transferred to the *Shrewsbury Chronicle*. A lot more was going on in the county town, but to his frustration most of his stories were cut to ribbons. Not because he was over-writing; everyone's copy was slashed. There was an acute shortage of newsprint in post-war Britain. The big dailies got the lion's share of what was available, with slim pickings left for their regional cousins. Sometimes a planned twelve-page edition was cut back at the last minute to just four. Painstakingly written articles and features were savagely subbed down or bit the dust entirely.

Dad grew sick of it. Everyone did. Then one day a colleague confided over a pint that he'd cracked the problem. He was taking a job in Canada.

'They've got newsprint coming out of their ears over there, Chris. You can't move for bloody trees in Canada. I've got a pal working on the *Toronto Star* – forty pages every edition! I'm off. You should give it some serious thought, too.'

Canada ... the place seemed increasingly bound up in Madeley destiny. It had never once occurred to Chris to go there, yet now it seemed the most obvious thing in the world to do.

Canada. There was no rationing, while shortages in Britain were getting worse by the week. There was even talk of bread being put on the points system. Bread! You wouldn't think we'd won the war . . .

As Chris rode his blaring motorbike back to Kiln Farm that evening, he could think of nothing but Canada. He had close relatives over there, so he wouldn't be quite alone. His father had loved his own days in Canada and spoke of them often; he'd only come back because of bloody William.

Since the end of the war his parents had made the first of many visits to Canada to see Geoffrey's family, while James took care of the farm. Chris was sure the Madeleys over there could put him up for a while.

By the time he was kicking out the stand on the Norton by the back door of the farmhouse, his mind was made up. He had some savings – more than enough for his fare. He was going.

He saw Geoffrey coming out of the dairy shed after the evening's milking. Chris hesitated a moment, then hurried across the farmyard to break the news to his father.

*

My father was fully aware that a strange family pattern was repeating itself as his ship was shepherded out of the River Mersey by Liverpool's pilot boats. As the liner's screws increased their revolutions and the famous Liver Birds sank below the horizon, he thought about Henry's family making exactly the same departure more than forty years before, and of Geoffrey's hopeful voyage to find them thirteen years later. He felt a squirm of excitement in his belly as he reflected that, like his father and grandfather before him, he was in his turn sailing due west towards the mouth of the great St Lawrence.

But these fathers and sons had crossed the Atlantic with different imperatives. Henry was escaping bankruptcy and ruin. Geoffrey was chasing the dream of being reunited with his long-lost family. Now Chris was turning his back on his own parents.

They had supported his decision to emigrate but he sensed something approaching regret as well. His father appeared more reluctant than Kitty to see his youngest son go, although it was hard to be sure. Geoffrey's emotions were as inscrutable as ever. Chris had been slightly confused; after all, his father forced him to go to Denstone. He genuinely thought he would be pleased to learn that his son was leaving Shawbury again, but Chris thought he could detect sadness in his father's voice when they talked over his plans.

Dad and I spoke about this years later, just a few months before he died. I was in no doubt. 'I think Granddad realised that deep down he loved you,' I told him. 'You can't compare going to Denstone with emigrating to Canada, Dad. No wonder he seemed upset. Given the way he knew he'd treated you he probably thought he'd never see you again.'

My father became quite thoughtful after this conversation. Later that evening, he did something almost unheard of. He telephoned Shawbury 'just for a chat' with his father.

It's never too late to salvage something from the wreckage.

Before setting sail for Quebec, Chris had been in touch with the Thomson newspaper group's Toronto office. They ran a string of titles over there and, after some hard lobbying, he was offered a reporter's job in the city. They'd found him digs near the offices; he was, his editor-to-be said in a telegram, 'all set'.

Bad weather in the mid-Atlantic slowed the ship down, as did an unusually heavy crop of icebergs off Newfoundland. When Chris's bus arrived in Toronto he was several days late.

He reported direct to his newspaper. The editor was in conference, he was told at the front desk. Come back in an hour.

He did so and after a long wait was shown into the deputy editor's office. It was empty.

Eventually a harassed-looking man in shirtsleeves and glasses hurried in. He shook hands with my father and offered him a cigarette.

'Good trip over?'

'Well, apart from the storms and some icebergs. That's why I'm a bit late. I –'

The other man waved expansively. 'Sure, sure, these things happen. I had to sail to London last year for the paper and the same thing happened to me. Missed my story. Almost lost my job, ha ha!'

There was an uncomfortable pause, and then the deputy took a deep breath and delivered the *coup de grâce*.

'See here, Madeley, it's like this. You're a newspaperman, you know how it works. A deadline is a deadline. You missed yours – not your fault – and . . . well, I'm afraid the job's gone to another guy. He's been pestering all hell out of us and . . .

well, he was around and you weren't. Sorry. Nothing personal.'

'I'm only three days late.'

'Three days is something of an eternity on a daily, friend. Like I said, I'm sorry.'

The interview was over and Chris found himself in an elevator going back down to the lobby. Half an hour before he thought he had a job and somewhere to live. Now he was literally out on the street.

To his credit, he didn't panic, though he felt horribly winded and humiliated. What would he tell his colleagues back home on the paper? Or his parents, come to that? Sacked before he'd even walked through the door.

He went to a drugstore, bought every newspaper in the place, traded some of his dwindling dollars for dimes and settled in for a long haul at the payphone. He had to get a job.

Perhaps a note of desperation had slipped into his voice, perhaps it was because he was calling from a public phone and had to keep inserting his coins as the pips sounded, but Chris received increasingly short shrift from the newspapers he dialled. He began to feel defeated even before he was put through to the editor, or more often, an assistant. After a while he hung up and went for a coffee. He wasn't going to land a reporter's job like this.

But damn it, he needed to find some kind of employment, fast. And somewhere to live. He toyed briefly with the idea of calling one of several relatives who lived in Ontario to beg a bed for a few nights, but he felt too ashamed and embarrassed. He had to fix this on his own.

He ended his first day in Toronto with the promise of a job selling men's underwear in a downtown department store, and a month's rent on a filthy bedsit across the city.

Far from home and jobless, Chris spent the evening exploring downtown Toronto. He had never seen anything like it, but the teeming Canadian city was too much for him that night. Far from being energised by the sight of soaring buildings, enormous, flashy cars, and the sound of voices speaking in what to him sounded like an authentic American twang (he would learn to distinguish the difference), he was intimidated. It was too much to absorb after such a terrible start and he gave up and took a bus to his digs, feeling utterly defeated.

Not exactly what he had come three and a half thousand miles for.

*

Most of us can remember a run of particularly bad luck in our lives or careers, or both. Now, fortune resolutely refused to shine on my father. It was partly bad timing on his part. Thousands of Canadian servicemen were being demobbed every month and understandably they got first pick of the jobs in what was, after all, their own country. Several times he was convinced he had landed a position in some newsroom only to be told at the last minute that a local man had belatedly entered the frame and taken priority.

It was the same in men's underwear. After a few weeks Chris was quietly let go in favour of a local man just out of the army.

Sometimes he took a bus into the tobacco country outside the city and earned a few dollars picking leaves in the harvest. He enjoyed this; it reminded him a little of home. It also reminded him that he couldn't afford to buy cigarettes any more. He was economising on food, too; photographs of him at this time show my father to be disturbingly gaunt.

But he was stranded. He had come to Canada optimistically on a one-way ticket, and going back home wasn't an option. Years later he would ruefully say to me: 'Never travel anywhere without your fare home in your back pocket. Not anywhere.'

By the autumn of 1950, he was in an extremely tight spot. The tobacco harvest was over and he was flat broke, reduced to patrolling the sands of Lake Ontario with his Leica camera – a twenty-first birthday present from his parents – taking photos of children on donkey rides and hustling their parents to buy them at a dollar a shot. Most politely declined. There was one compensation; he was fascinated by the Great Lakes, giant freshwater expanses so wide that their opposite shores lay far below the horizon. They seemed more like oceans than lakes, and when the donkeys were resting he took wonderful seascapes with his Leica purely for his own pleasure.

Then, out of the blue, his beach-bum existence threw him a break.

It was a warm October afternoon and a large, prosperous family had gathered on the sands. The father was dressed in an immaculate tan suit, his pretty wife in a spreading dress cinched in tightly at the waist. Their children were in cool crisp cotton and a uniformed nanny and a chauffeur fussed in attendance. The glamorous party appeared to be waiting for someone to show up.

My father drifted over.

'Goddamned reporters,' growled the paterfamilias, glaring around him. 'Where the hell are they? I told 'em, three o'clock at the pier.'

Chris's scalp tingled as he felt the electric crackle of opportunity.

'Excuse me . . . I'm a newspaperman. Freelance. I write, and I take photos. Can I be of help?'

The other man looked the scarecrow up and down, and then grinned. 'You sure can, limey. My company's just taken over a coupla big employers in Sault Ste Marie and Tillsonburg. Saved a lot of jobs. Big story. Local papers want pictures of the saviour of Ontario and his family, but it looks like their reporters can't follow directions worth a damn.'

He fished in his pocket and pulled out a list of newspaper titles.

'Here they are – all syndicated. Just send your shots and words to them. Think you can do it? We gotta be outta here in five minutes.'

Dad grabbed his pictures, dashed down some quotes, and headed for the darkroom of a sympathetic friend, a more successful freelance photographer who shared his tenement block, allowed him to borrow.

He was back in business.

*

It was tales like this that led me into journalism. I found my father's accounts of his days in penury in Toronto rather glamorous. I was excited by the casino-like game of chance and luck involved in breaking into the newspaper business, and admired my father's stubborn refusal to accept persistent rejection.

Later, I learned that setbacks like his are common among journalists. Everyone has a tale to tell. One of my first editors was, as a young reporter, desperate to work on America's west coast. In 1963 he wangled an interview for a job on the *Los Angeles Times* and arrived at its headquarters on a late autumn day with a well-rehearsed pitch.

He turned up on time outside the editor's office, but something was wrong. Sobbing could be heard from up and down the corridor; the great man's secretary's cheeks ran with mascara.

'I'm sorry,' she sniffled, 'but our president's just been shot.'

He cursed himself for skipping his research on the corporate structure of the *LA Times* and made sympathetic noises. The editor materialised and called him in.

'Hi, Bob. Look, I'm sorry, but this meeting's gonna have to wait. Our president's just been shot dead.'

My future boss decided to play it straight. 'Yes, I heard . . . I'm so sorry . . . er . . . what was his name?'

Three hours later he was on a plane home, probably the only British journalist to leave America on the day everyone else was swarming in. To cover the assassination of President Kennedy.

My dad loved that story. Meanwhile, back in 1950 Toronto,

he worked his beach break for all it was worth. There was a central pool for syndicated copy but he bypassed that, calling each paper in turn and insisting on speaking with the editor. He offered to write subtly different stories for each title so it looked like they'd had a staff man on the job, and sent a series of alternative photos to the picture desks too, so they could claim exclusives.

He was by-lined in some editions and by the end of the day had landed a contract as a reporter/photographer for the *Woodstock Sentinel Review*, Tillsonburg bureau. Tillsonburg was a medium-sized tobacco town ninety miles southwest of Toronto and about twelve miles from the shores of Lake Erie.

My father's break would lead to an encounter with a red-headed, eighteen-year-old actress.

My mother.

*

The *Woodstock Sentinel Review* was an even smaller outfit than the *Whitchurch Herald*. But at least Chris was a big fish in a small pond. Well, a middling fish in a minuscule pond. He was a one-man band, reporting on all the news and sport fit to cover. The pay wasn't great, but enough for him to run a car, rent a decent apartment and start buying his packs of Winchesters again.

Compared to life in grey, pinched, exhausted, rationed-to-the-hilt, bankrupted post-war England, Canada was a land flowing with milk and honey. This part of Ontario rubbed up close and cosy against its border with America. Nearby

Windsor looked across narrow straits to giant Detroit; US prosperity spilled into its neighbour's garden like water from an overflowing lake.

Sometimes Chris's news beat took him to bigger towns nearby – London, Hamilton and Detroit's Canadian twin, Windsor. He couldn't get used to the sights that surrounded him. Everything was off the scale. Huge, shiny, gas-guzzling American cars (not that their thirstiness mattered – petrol was plentiful at just a few cents a gallon). Soda parlours offering every flavour of ice cream human imagination could devise. Drive-in movie theatres with little private speakers you hooked over your car's windows. Ice-hockey rinks, brilliantly lit for violent night-time clashes between armour-clad warriors who smashed into each other, the baying crowd not satisfied until bright-red blood was sprayed across the slashed and scarred ice. Extravagantly floodlit baseball games with pitchers and batters worshipped like gods by their roaring fans.

There were chromed and mirrored bars, their walls lined with bottles of spirits bearing names he'd never even heard of. Hamburger joints, serving enormous patties of prime beef that were worth a month's meat ration back home. Customers usually managed to eat about half of them. The rest was simply thrown away. Thrown away!

And television. Everyone had a television, the programmes impossibly superior to the modest transmissions Chris had occasionally glimpsed on the flickering sets still rare in England. Proper shows that everyone watched and talked and laughed about the next day. Many were piped in direct from the States. *The Ed Sullivan Show*, live from New York – urbane, witty, modern. *The Sid Caesar Show* – side-splittingly funny. Apparently teams of writers worked on these programmes, roomfuls of men slaving to produce comedy jewels. Then there were the news shows; not formal, tight-sphinctered bulletins like the BBC's clipped announcements, but rollicking, rolling extravaganzas of news and unabashed comment, stuffed with on-the-spot footage and hosted by charismatic men who were stars and household names in their own right. And all of it peppered with brash commercials, sponsors' messages and cinema-style trailers for forthcoming programmes.

It was dazzling; amazing. Chris felt he had travelled through space and time and had landed in a futuristic nirvana.

Then there was the weather. Shawbury's extremes seemed like mild fluctuations compared with what happened here. Summer was insufferably hot and humid; as humid as Florida, some said, with more mosquitoes. It was because of the moisture from the Great Lakes virtually surrounding the huge inland peninsular, the same watery expanses that in winter produced unimaginable quantities of snow. Lake snow, they called it. One could draw the bedroom curtains on a dry, clear, frosty night and open them next morning to look out on a different planet. Not the few inches of fluffily decorous white Chris remembered from home, but a vast shape-shifting shroud, feet thick. Familiar neighbourhood landmarks entirely vanished; road signs, hedges, walls and parked cars buried beneath the earth's shining new crust.

Tillsonburg and its surrounding tobacco farms may have been a small news beat but it wasn't quiet. Whatever went on there was my father's job to cover. He soon became fluent in the mysteries of ice hockey, baseball, basketball, and Little League or Pee-Wee. Locals liked the tall Englishman with his funny accent and he started making friends. Photographs from this time show him still at his underfed skinniest, but relaxed and smiling. His trademark spectacles gave him something of a Clark Kent appearance. He looked quite different without them. In later life, people used to say that when he removed his glasses he was a ringer for the actor Robert Wagner. He would pretend to be surprised, but secretly he was flattered by the comparison. After all, Wagner was partnered with the gorgeous Stephanie Powers in the global TV hit *Hart to Hart*.

One of Dad's new friends was a fellow newspaperman called Bill. He was the editor of the *Tillsonburg News*, a guy on the up-and-up. Bill drove a big red Pontiac and reportedly had a stunning girlfriend. One day he phoned Chris to beg a favour.

'Chris, I'm on a story in Toronto tonight. I promised I'd walk my girl home from the theatre – she's starring in that new play at the Town Hall. Would you be her knight in shining armour for me?'

'Of course. What's she called?'

'Mary Claire. Mary Claire McEwan. I'll tell her to look out for the beanpole in the foyer. Be there around ten. Thanks, pal.'

'Wait. How will I know her?'

A laugh at the other end. 'You'll know her.'

Dad was slightly delayed by a story that evening and arrived at the theatre a few minutes after ten. Most of the audience and cast had already left but as he ran up the steps to the foyer the doors opened and a petite, red-headed girl hurried out. Chris thought she looked a knockout and rather French in her smart belted raincoat.

'Mary Claire?'

'Yes. If you're Chris, you're late.'

'I know, I'm sorry . . . I got stuck on a story.'

'Hmm. You sound like Bill.'

'Er . . . yes . . . well, I'm here now. Shall we go?'

'What do you think I was just doing?'

My father worked hard to make up lost ground as they walked to her parents' house. After a few minutes he managed to make her laugh, and flattered her by asking about the play. But suddenly she interrupted him with: 'We're here.'

They were standing in front of a frame house that faced the town cinema. Two flights of wooden steps led to a veranda and front door. Through a window he could see a woman moving about. That must be Mrs McEwan, Chris thought.

He couldn't hide his disappointment that they had arrived. 'So soon? But I was hoping . . .'

'What, that I have to walk halfway across town every night? Sorry, Englishman, this is the end of the line.'

He played for time. 'Look, about the play. I'd like to come and see it. I could write a review for the paper, and use a picture of you. How would that be?'

'That would be . . . very nice. Thank you. Bill's been promising to do the same thing since we opened.'

'Then I'll see you tomorrow. Goodnight.'

'Night.'

My father slowly retraced his steps, thinking about how he would describe this girl in his article. If he'd known how she was describing him to her mother at that very moment, he probably would have passed out with shock.

'Play go well, dear? Want some coffee? There's some still on, I think.'

'Yes, it went fine. Thanks, I'll take a cup.'

'Bill walk you home again?'

'No, he's out of town. One of his friends did. An Englishman.'

'Oh? What's he like?'

Mary Claire sipped her coffee.

'I think we're going to be married.'

*

She brought him home for dinner a week after they met. This first meal with her family, such a timeless, prosaic ritual on the surface, was in fact one of the great turning points of my father's life. It would have an immeasurable impact on him and his attitude to fatherhood, and a profound effect on my own childhood.

I owe a lot to the clan McEwan. But they couldn't lay all of Christopher's ghosts. Some bad spirits have a tendency to linger.

Chapter 7

———

LAYING GHOSTS

Chris had been so busy making his way in the world that for nearly four years he had managed to push Denstone and his complete failure to form a demonstrative, loving relationship with his father to the bottom of his thoughts.

But nothing is forever buried. He was still emotionally scarred. Deep down he secretly thought there must be something fundamentally wrong with him. If not, why had his parents sent him away? He must be intrinsically unlovable, he decided. That was why his attempts to forge a bond with Geoffrey had never got anywhere. If his own father couldn't bring himself to show the slightest affection towards him, well . . . he, Chris, couldn't be worth very much, could he? The bleak logic seemed inescapable.

Four years chasing other people's stories had deferred the reckoning and bought him some time; formed an anaesthetised buffer zone between childhood and manhood. But

---

now his suppressed insecurities began rising to the surface. Although this whirlwind romance with Mary Claire had shaken his heart – he was completely in love with her – how could she possibly love him in return? It could only be a matter of time before she caught on to the fact he was unlovable.

Gradually my mother began to sense a deep well of self-doubt concealed behind her fiancé's outwardly confident manner. She perceived that his Englishness provided him with a screen to hide behind. Englishmen were famous for their emotional reticence, she knew, so at first it wasn't surprising to her that when she asked him about his childhood and parents he was not exactly evasive, but reserved and vague.

Oh, he was open enough about the factual elements of his past. She knew his parents' names, where they lived, where Chris had gone to school and so on.

But one evening, after the two of them had said their goodnights, she reflected on the conversation they'd had over dinner, and suddenly grasped what was missing from it.

He never spoke about his feelings. Not regarding his boyhood, anyway. Not about the past at all, in fact. With a slight shock she realised she had no idea if he had been a happy child or not, or what he thought of his parents. He simply didn't say. More to the point, he avoided saying. What could it mean?

As the months went by, the studied casualness he always displayed over these matters began to unsettle her. She confided in her mother Barbara.

'It's not that I believe he's hiding something horrible,

Mother. I don't think he has some awful dark secret or anything like that. But I can tell he's unsure and unhappy about something, and I'm more and more certain it's somehow to do with his family in England. I want to help him but I don't know what to say or do.'

Barbara regarded her eldest daughter calmly. 'You must get him completely on his own, choose your moment, and ask him outright. You'll get your answer, dear – either by what he says, or what he doesn't say.'

The following weekend Chris, on Mary Claire's suggestion, hired a small motor launch and the two of them went out for the day on Lake Erie. It was now humid, sultry summer but they were cooled by the breeze puffing across the water. They ate their lunch as the little boat rocked in the slight swell of the great inland sea, and after a long companionable silence, Mary Claire decided the moment had come.

'Darling . . . what is it you won't tell me about your childhood, your life back at Shawbury?'

Years later my father would describe the question as like a door swinging open before him; a doorway he could shun or pass through. The choice was his.

He turned to look towards the distant shoreline, and then back at the eyes of the young woman looking solemnly into his own. The moment held itself in perfect balance a while longer and then gently dipped under his decision.

'Well . . . this will probably sound . . . I don't know. I've never spoken to a soul about it, but . . .'

For the first time in his life, hesitatingly, Chris began to describe the doubts and fears and disappointments that had haunted him for as long as he could remember. As his fiancée listened in silence, the lake murmured its accompaniment.

A dark tide that had begun to run nearly half a century earlier, flooding through two lives, father's and son's, was at last about to turn.

*

Chris's childhood was, to Mary Claire, a bewildering contrast to her own happy, freewheeling Canadian upbringing. She could see at once that her future father-in-law had been savagely assaulted by fate, but her concern now was to free his son from what seemed to her like something close to a curse. She realised the young man she had agreed to marry had had no working model, no template, on which to base their future family life together.

So the McEwans unselfconsciously presented him with their own example. It was to be his salvation. And, ultimately, up to a point, mine.

*

Mary Claire's kid brother Bailey was barely a fortnight old when Chris walked into my mother's family home at 174 Broadway for the first time. Her younger sister Barbara-Ann was fifteen. Mary Claire was eighteen, and the oldest child, Malcolm, twenty-two. Their mother, Barbara, was in her early forties and father Hector had just turned fifty. It was a vibrant family that cheerfully spanned five decades; a typical and triumphant product of the modern North American way – confident, affluent (Hector owned a garage and Barbara ran a hair salon), forward-looking and relaxed.

Chris had never been in a house like it. The McEwan home seemed to glow with emotional warmth. Perhaps that was because women were a strong presence – a mother and two daughters outnumbered and outgunned the men and Chris marvelled at the loving, playful atmosphere that surged around him whenever he visited his fiancée. He didn't realise it then, but his emotional DNA was being subtly re-engineered by the McEwans' family chemistry. Their immediate unfeigned fondness for him astounded him. These were people who spontaneously kissed and hugged each other, and the young Englishman found himself the new object of their warm familiarity.

My father told me he experienced more demonstrative affection in one week in Tillsonburg than he had known in his entire life in Shawbury. At first he was startled and confused by the experience; quickly he came to love it. And them.

My father was most fascinated by Hector's behaviour. On weekend visits to the McEwan home, Dad would sit pretending to read a newspaper while covertly observing his future father-in-law's playful exchanges with his children as they came and went. Malcolm, though now in his early twenties, was still hugged, kissed or playfully wrestled with. Chris was astounded. Watching such overt demonstrations of affection was almost like learning a new language.

The girls were kissed and teased too, and Bailey was everyone's darling, swept through the house in the interchangeable arms of his siblings or parents. If the baby had been an accidental and tardy addition to the family, he was clearly a welcome one.

It is impossible to overemphasise the critical importance of this period for my father. It may have been very late in the day, and his epiphany came not a moment too soon, but he was being presented with a model lesson in how to play happy families. Demonstrably, showing and receiving love and affection was normal. The more he observed it, the easier it looked. And not only that: the little clan on Broadway continued to make their growing affection for him abundantly plain. Mary Claire had confided in her mother and Barbara went out of her way to make the young Englishman feel loved and welcomed into the family. His confidence soared.

It was wonderful. It was a revelation. It was, as I say, my father's salvation. But he still carried his interior scars. They would never be completely healed.

*

Chris and Mary Claire were married in Tillsonburg on 13 October 1951. The bridegroom was twenty-three, the bride nineteen. He cocked up his wedding vows, saying: 'I hereby troth thee my plight' and she was not allowed even a thimbleful of champagne at the reception. Mary Claire was old enough to get married but, under Canada's strict alcohol prohibitions, too young to drink.

She was old enough to bear children too. My mother fell pregnant almost at once and ten months later gave birth to a daughter – Elizabeth Barbara Madeley. Telegrams were sent: mother and baby doing fine.

But the father wasn't. Chris was still desperately thin and working extra shifts for his newspaper to earn enough to keep his little family. He was exhausted after eighteen-hour days and seemed to have no resistance to infections. Heavy smoking didn't help and after a vicious bout of bronchitis his new wife took charge.

'We can't carry on like this, Chris. You're going to wear yourself out. You *are* worn out. And Elizabeth and I hardly ever see you. We have to think of something else.'

My father nodded. 'All right. But what? It took me months to get the job I have now.'

The couple both had aunts living in Windsor, the big industrial city which stared across the border into America and 'Motown' – Detroit. My mother considered this a while, and then seized the moment.

'Let's go to Windsor – today, right now. There's plenty of work there and we can stay with our aunts while we get fixed up.'

And so my slightly bewildered father found himself catching the last train from Tillsonburg that evening with his wife and baby, headed for the US border and Windsor, Ontario. Next morning the couple walked into the city's Employment Centre and walked out with job interviews at the giant Ford of Canada plant. An hour later they were on the payroll – Mary Claire was assigned to production planning, Chris, with his journalistic experience, to the communications department, in effect, the press office. He would work for Ford in public relations until the day he died.

Once again Mary Claire was my father's saviour. With kinder hours and better pay he began finally to put on some weight, and he was energised and uplifted by the turn their lives had taken.

He also had more time to spend getting to know his growing daughter. My mother says he was an infinitely gentle, tender father. Like all new fathers he had to feel his way, but he had very little experience from his own childhood to call on. He had to rely on what he'd learned in the McEwan family home. That, as it turned out, served well enough.

But my mother says he seemed to have an instinct for it anyway. Becoming a father was enormously important to him. I think he felt fatherhood, and marriage, defined him properly for the first time in his life.

But, as well as learning to define himself, Chris was also attempting to define his wife. She had harboured thoughts of returning to the stage, but he wouldn't hear of it. Today, we might call his attitude 'controlling'.

My father met my mother when she was playing the female lead in a light romantic comedy, and it had involved some stage kisses. This was all very well then; now she was his wife, he could not bear the thought of her in the arms of another man. And it might not just be as part of a local amateur production – a casting agent who had seen my mother's work wanted to represent her professionally. Who knew where that might lead? And with whom?

It would not be the first time in her marriage that Mary Claire was forced to ponder the implications of her wedding-day vow to 'obey' her husband.

Mostly, the pledge was not invoked. But occasionally my father's insecurities surfaced and he restricted her. It was an issue that affected many women of my mother's generation, and one that would not be confronted until the rise of feminism.

So she renounced any remaining ambitions to pursue a theatrical career, telling friends she was happy to be a wife and mother. Although this was not without a large degree of truth, there was definitely an element of pretence. Years later, when she wanted to drive, my father refused to allow it, even though she had passed her test as a teenager in Canada and was confident she would pass a UK examination. My mother told everyone that it was a matter of cost, but again this was only partly true. The main issue was her husband's superstitious fear that a driving wife might just one day drive away from him for good.

She was quite unable to reassure him that this was nonsense, any more than she had been able to convince him she had no intention of running off with her next leading man. Her eventual response was to accede gracefully to his demand. Recently I asked her why.

'It was partly the times, Richard,' she told me. 'Things were just . . . different for women like me then. But also I simply didn't want to make him unhappy.

'Yes, I wanted to act and I wanted to drive – quite badly sometimes – but not *that* badly, you see. We were so happy together and, anyway, I'd known he was insecure when I married him, hadn't I? He'd told me everything. I loved that I had managed to take some of that insecurity away and make him stronger. Why would I want to endanger that?'

I hope he knew how lucky he was. I think so.

*

If Chris looked out of his new office window he could see straight into the smokestacks of mighty Detroit across the narrows that marked the Canadian–US border. He began to think about transferring to America. The pay was better, opportunities were greater . . . why not?

Because of my mother's teeth.

Mary Claire cleared away her husband's supper plate in the kitchen of their little flat in Windsor, checked the baby – now more of a toddler – was still asleep, and cleared her throat. She had been dreading this conversation since getting the news that afternoon, but it had to be had.

'Darling . . . you know I went to the dentist today.'

'Sure, honey.' After several years in Canada, Chris now spoke in an unaffected North American accent.

'Well . . . it's not good news.'

'What? You're not ill with something, are you?'

Mary Claire shook her head. 'No, it's not anything serious . . . just expensive. He told me I have to have all my teeth out – *all* of them, Chris – and have false ones made and it's going to cost a thousand dollars!' She burst into tears.

Chris was aghast. 'But of course that's serious! We haven't got a thousand dollars. We haven't got a hundred dollars.

Christ, it'd be cheaper to take a boat to England and get you fixed on the National Health!'

Mary Claire looked up. 'You're not serious.'

'Well, no . . . I mean, yes, it's true, we could get you seen to for free in England, but I didn't mean . . . I wasn't actually suggesting . . .'

They stared at each other. Mary Claire spoke first.

'There's many a true word spoken in jest. I think you might be on to something. Let's sleep on it, shall we?'

And so it was that at the beginning of August 1954 my parents and their two-year-old daughter boarded the *Empress of France* at Montreal. They were to stay in England for a year, as an experiment. It seemed silly to go all that way just for a visit to the dentist. Maybe they might like to settle there.

The *Empress of France* cast off, bound for Liverpool. But Liverpool was not their final destination.

My father was taking his young family home.

Back to Kiln Farm.

*

The voyage got off to an exciting start. With Elizabeth safely asleep in their cabin, the couple went on deck to watch the tugs tow the liner out into the St Lawrence River. Chris wanted to take photographs of them but his wife kept standing in his way. Finally, in mock frustration, he grasped her by the waist and pretended he was about to throw her overboard.

The strange woman wearing near-identical clothes to Mary Claire struggled free. 'What *do* you think you're doing?'

Chris gaped in horror. 'Oh, I'm so sorry . . . I thought you were my wife.'

That's how Dad used to tell it, anyway; my mother insists he only shouted in mock anger at the woman, thinking it was her. Either way, both agreed that the stranger never let my mother out of her sight whenever she came on deck. She clearly thought she was in mortal danger from a homicidal husband.

As I say, the decision to sail for England was not based solely on Mary Claire's dental dilemma. Once the initial idea had taken root other reasons surfaced. Britain was finally moving out of years of austerity; rationing was almost at an end and after four years away Chris realised he was homesick. Mary Claire, though nervous about emigrating and convinced she would miss her mother terribly (indeed she did – they wrote to each other every single day and the entire McEwan clan came over from Tillsonburg to visit) had long been something of an Anglophile and was intensely curious to see the country of her husband's birth.

The decision was sealed by the news that Ford had an opening in their British press office. The job was Chris's if he wanted it.

It seemed like fate.

*

My mother remembers that their ship docked in Liverpool on 8 August. When she told me this during my research for this book, I gently corrected her.

'No, Mum, the eighth of August is the date Dad died.'

There was a pause. 'Yes it was,' she said, her Canadian accent thickening as it always does at emotional moments. 'But it was also the date I landed with him in England all those years before. Good Lord. It never struck me until now. How strange.'

My father never returned to Canada. Neither, during their marriage, did his wife, except to be at her mother's bedside ten years later when she died.

Less than two years after arriving in Britain, my mother gave birth to me. Chris now had a son, and a slew of renewed self-doubt assailed him.

He had, over the previous four years, been a gentle and loving father to his daughter. Indeed, against all his expectations, he had found fatherhood relatively easy. His epiphany at the McEwan home had stood him in good stead; Chris had learned his lessons there well.

But what if this were different? What if it was different with sons? What if all that rejection and emotional frigidity with his father had tainted him in some way? What if the cold past returned to warp and chill the relationship with his own boy?

All his old doubts and fears and uncertainties rushed back. Poor Dad.

I can conjure up his pale face now, staring at his reflection in the shaving mirror the morning after I was born, a question running through his head just as it had Geoffrey's more than thirty years before, when Kitty presented him with their first child.

But the question troubling Christopher was subtly different. He had so far succeeded in being a good father – to his daughter. But now there was a son in his house. What sort of a father would he make to him?

Chapter 8

———

ESSEX BOY

The Shropshire Madeleys arrived in force at Liverpool to greet their wandering son and his new bride and child. It was practically a committee that stood patiently on the wharf waiting for the *Empress of France* to disgorge its passengers. Geoffrey and Kitty were there, as was Chris's elder brother Jim, with his new wife Hilda. Hilda was very pretty, with brown curls, astonishingly bright eyes and very neat white teeth. She came from Market Drayton and she and Jim had married after Chris had emigrated. Both brothers would shortly be meeting the other's new bride for the first time.

Meanwhile, in the unloading sheds opposite, Chris and Mary Claire's luggage – everything they had in the world – had vanished without trace and their little girl was flushed and unwell. My mother, weak from calamitous seasickness which had plagued her during the entire voyage, recognised her in-laws from photographs but her husband had disappeared in

---

pursuit of their missing trunks and she was too nervous to approach her new family alone.

One of them gave an uncertain wave of half-recognition. She burst into tears and fled to the back of the shed.

Later, after the drive down to Shawbury, Elizabeth, who had been increasingly restless, suddenly went into a sharp decline. The doctor was called out. His diagnosis seemed strangely and ominously fateful. On this, her very first night at Kiln Farm, Elizabeth had been struck down by precisely the same illness that had stolen John from his parents nearly thirty years before – bronchial pneumonia. The little girl was even lying in the same bedroom where the small boy had been propped up on his pillows the night before he died. A frisson of superstitious dread rippled through everyone.

But this was the 1950s, not the 1920s. My sister was trans-ferred, semi-conscious, to Shrewsbury Hospital where she was placed in an oxygen tent and fed antibiotics. Modern medicine duly carried the day and the family managed to shrug off the sense that dark and malign forces were at work.

But no one actually mentioned John by name.

Geoffrey and Kitty had missed their youngest boy more keenly than their letters to him ever showed. Kitty was the chief letter writer, and Chris had received a steady stream of blue airmail envelopes containing news from Kiln Farm while he was in Canada. The letters from home were mostly factual, concerned with goings-on in the village and how the crops were doing. Sometimes there might be a scrawled paragraph from Geoffrey, but no clue from either parent how much they wanted to see their youngest son again. Now, they insisted he and his wife stay at Kiln Farm for at least a month before he started his new job at Ford's headquarters in Dagenham, Essex. So my mother had an opportunity to become familiar with this emotionally charged parcel of land, and to get to know her husband's parents.

Years later, Geoffrey would confess to her that, at first, the arrival of his son's Canadian wife had confused and unsettled him. It brought back memories of The Girl. He had been unable to persuade his first fiancé to sail to England with him, but Chris had successfully brought his own girl home. My grandfather admired this, and also my mother's determination to make the journey, leaving her own family behind.

My mother certainly made an impact on Shawbury. Her red hair and glamorous looks marked her out. She dressed in the tailored, fashionable clothes she had brought with her to a country still emerging from the so-called Age of Austerity. Because of the height difference with her husband – she was five-foot four to his six-foot two – she always wore high heels. The whole combined to produce a distinctly chic, Parisian look. This, and her distinctive Canadian accent, caused heads to turn in the village shop.

She made an impact on Geoffrey too. He quickly became fond of my mother, and it was the beginning of a friendship which, in later years, saw him increasingly confide in her on the long walks they took through the countryside; conversations she remembers to this day and which were of enormous value in the writing of this book.

Now, at last, my mother saw for herself the stage upon which her husband's childhood had been played out. She walked gingerly around the bomb crater in the first field and shuddered to see how close to the house it was. She inspected the stables where Captain had once whinnied for my father, now home to diesel-stinking tractors. She fished for trout on the bend in the river where Kitty's ducks had sailed away on a long-ago summer's afternoon. One wet August day, Chris borrowed his father's Morris and drove her across country to Denstone. After ten minutes walking around the empty school – the 'hols' were not yet over – she quietly asked to be driven back. She could see her husband was becoming increasingly agitated. And seeing it through Chris's eyes, she thought it a loathsome place.

After a week or two spent settling in, Chris drove Mary Claire into Shrewsbury for her long-dreaded appointment with the Madeley family dentist.

She was ushered into the surgery. My mother shivered at the sight of the ancient pre-war dental equipment: a huge drilling rig with flapping drive belts connected to foot pedals; an array of obscure but terrifying instruments Queen Victoria would probably have recognised; and bottles of what looked suspiciously like chloroform or ether.

She wished heartily that she had stayed on the other side of the Atlantic and had all her teeth pulled under gas in a modern North American dentist's. The British National Health may be saving a thousand dollars, but she felt like she had walked into a torture chamber.

Outside, her husband sat in the waiting room flicking through a tattered copy of *Punch*, dating from around the time of Munich. He was expecting a lengthy vigil – most of the afternoon – but suddenly the surgery door opened and my mother walked through, smiling, holding a slightly bloodied rag to a corner of her mouth.

'What's happened, Claire? You can't possibly have had all of them removed already.'

"On't need 'oo,' she answered indistinctly through the cloth before taking it away for a moment. 'He says there's nothing wrong with my teeth, except one or two at the back that were crowding the others. One more treatment and I'm fixed. That guy in Windsor was a chiseller, Chris, out for a fast buck.'

On the drive back to Kiln Farm, Chris glanced across at his wife. 'Well, Claire . . . it looks like we needn't have come to England after all, doesn't it?'

'Looks like it.'

There was a pause before my father spoke again.

'D'you mind?'

My mother shook her head. 'No, I don't think I do. You know I always wanted to visit England. Let's look on it as an adventure; see how things work out.'

For a moment my father couldn't speak. Then he managed a piece of understatement that was typical of him. 'OK . . . well, good. Thank you.'

My mother flashed him a quick smile. 'Nope, thank *you*. Well, your dentist anyway, in spite of that horrible medieval equipment he used. It's thanks to him I'll keep my teeth. And going by that lamb we had for lunch at the Fox and Hounds yesterday – it *was* lamb, wasn't it, Chris – I'm going to need them.'

*

By the autumn of that year my father was living in digs nearly 200 miles south of wife and child, working for the Yankee dollar. He was a public relations officer for Ford at their sprawling Dagenham plant and this enforced separation was something he and Mary Claire swiftly agreed could not be tolerated. Geoffrey loaned them the deposit on a semi standing on a busy main road in Romford, Essex, and by Christmas the young family was in residence. It looked as if the young couple were putting down permanent roots.

Later the following year, Mary Claire fell pregnant again. Essex boy was on his way.

*

The sight of flowering laburnum always reminds me that my birthday is approaching. When I was small my mother would point to the bursting yellow buds on the fine tree that stood outside our back door and whisper, 'See the petals? It means your birthday's coming.'

I was a Sunday's child, arriving on 13 May in the front room of our house in Dagenham Road, Rush Green. Rush Green had once been a small village outside the market town of Romford, but by 1956 it was almost entirely absorbed by a rapidly expanding post-war London. Traces of the countryside remained, though. Even today patches of ancient farmland survive around Romford, ploughed fields sitting bravely alongside 1930s-built housing estates and rows of shops and pubs. There are farmhouses still there too, some barely more than a stone's throw from the house where I was born: Crown

Farm; Warren Farm; Mill Farm . . . their outbuildings and fields make an incongruous sight for drivers surging down the dual carriageway that links the built-up suburbs stretching from Romford to the East End.

Later, when I was old enough to appreciate Kiln Farm's rural appeal, these fragments of countryside that stubbornly refused to be completely swamped by bricks and concrete held a deep attraction for me. I would ride my bike around their cement-besieged perimeters, closing my ears to the roar of traffic and resolutely turning my gaze towards the narrow vistas still free of cityscape. It was then that I first realised the hold Kiln Farm had begun to exert over me, even as a young boy. As time went by, I increasingly yearned for its meadows and trees and river, the red-bricked barns and outbuildings. I still do.

My father's reaction to the birth of his first son was extravagant. In the weeks after my birth my mother felt quite left in the shade. Chris would race home from Dagenham as fast as his wheezing pre-war Ford 8 would carry him, let himself in by the front door, and without so much as a 'Hi honey, I'm home' charge up the stairs to the nursery (well, the little box room at the back of the house) to stare and stare and stare at me if I were asleep, or pick me up and cradle me in his arms if I were even drowsily awake.

My mother admits to becoming quite jealous. 'You want your husband to love his new son, but you don't want to be usurped by him,' she told me candidly. It was sometimes over half an hour before her husband would sheepishly make his entrance downstairs and bid his wife and four-year-old daughter good evening.

More than half a century on from these exorbitant home-comings, I believe my father was plainly overcompensating. He was making it transparently clear to everyone – most of all, to himself – that the relationship with his son would not be anything like the one his father had had with him. And he was going to establish the difference right here and now. I was just a nappy-clad, speechless bundle of primary needs, but my father was determined to set the ground rules straight from the start. He was going to have a demonstrative, loving relationship with his son come hell or high water. Even if that meant, initially, exaggerating or even acting the role of a devoted father.

Was he acting? Not in the sense that he artfully concealed an absence of love. I think he was simply terrified of straying into that cold, neutral zone he and Geoffrey had inhabited together (and still did) and wanted to build a place where he could have a warm, open relationship with his son.

I love him very much for that. He'd thought about it. He reversed the flow. Henry, William, Geoffrey . . . they had all, in their own ways, done so much damage. Christopher had suffered enough and learned enough to be able to work out how to repair it.

My first memory is a very early one. I am lying in my pram, gazing up at a blue sky through the branches of a tree laden with white blossom. Some of the petals are fluttering down on to my face and I am watching them intently as they drift towards me. I can be scarcely more than one, and I must be under the old pear tree at the bottom of the garden where on sunny days I was parked for a nap.

Before the betrayal. The Madeleys, Worcester, circa 1902. Henry stands, hand on Geoffrey's chair. The rest of the family, left to right, are Doris, Hannah (with William on her knee), John and Douglas.

Father and sons, Shawbury
Church, circa 1935. Left to
right, Christopher, Geoffrey
and James.

Family at the gate, Kiln
Farm, mid-1950s. From 2nd
left, Christopher, Mary-
Claire, Jim, Kitty and
Geoffrey.

Dad on the crossing to Canada, 1950.

Dad's Canadian Club look – straight up, on the rocks.

Dad the journalist.

One of my father's early shots of his fiancée.

My parents' wedding day, 13 October 1951. Dad looks like he could do with eating all the cake, doesn't he?

The Brylcreem boys with the Madeleys' first car, second hand, of course. All my sister wanted were her second teeth.

Happy birthday, son. Now we are eight, in Epping Forest.

Dad – a dedicated gadget man – tries out his new remote camera. But why is he the only one looking at it?

Dad and me in Kitty's vegetable patch. We're on holiday, but Chris is still suited and booted.

Geoffrey and me at my sister Elizabeth's wedding, June 1977.

The twins at around the time I became 'steppie'. Tom is on the left, Dan on the right.

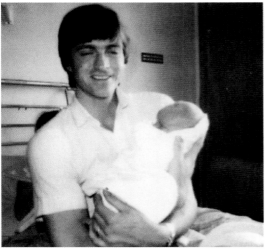

With Jack a few minutes after his birth, 19 May 1986.

The extended family. Judy and me on our wedding day, 21 November 1986, with, left to right, Dan, Tom and Jack.

Father and son, 2008.

The next break in the blank void of recall also involves blossom. My mother and I are looking through a window at the brilliant yellow petals on our laburnum tree. She points to it, and turns and smiles at me. 'Four tomorrow!'

Now my father drifts into view. He is always in a suit and tie. Always. And never in a shirt of any shade other than brilliant white, except when he was wearing his pyjamas. The first thing he put on in the morning was his spectacles; the lenses in heavy, black plastic frames, almost as dark as his thick hair which he slicked back with Brylcreem after shaving. I climbed into my parents' bed most mornings and watched the daily ritual of them dressing for the day. My mother first, facing into the wardrobe as she modestly fastens her bra. She swivels the cups round to her back while she fiddles with the clasp. The rigid, wired cones point at me from her shoulder blades and I confusedly think that ladies must have two pairs of breasts, one on the front and one at the back.

My father is invariably reading the paper in bed. It must have been the *Express* because I remember being fascinated by the helmeted knight who always guards the front page. 'Who is he?' I would ask my father.

'He's a Crusader. A very special soldier in days of old who fought for Jesus.'

'On his own?'

'No, he had his friends with him.'

And so on.

On Saturdays my mother had the afternoon 'off' after spending all week looking after house, husband and children. She usually went into Romford market – it was still a drovers market then, with flocks of bleating sheep – and browsed among the stalls, or admired the displays of crystal and cut glass in the department stores, while my father entertained my sister and me.

We might walk past the gasworks to Cottons Park where there were two slides, one of them breathtakingly high and steep with a wooden hut at the top to stop children falling off, the other disappointingly low and tame. Elizabeth, four years older than me, was allowed to swoop down the 'daddy' slide while I was confined to the baby version. I argued, begged and pleaded to be allowed to scale the metal Everest with my sister. The answer was always the same.

'Not until you're six.'

Or we would go out for a drive. The ancient Ford 8 was long gone and we had upgraded to another sit-up-and-beg economy car, the Popular. My father was very proud of this, his first new Ford. It was shiny jet-black with red upholstery and not much else – no heater (hot-water bottles and blankets on winter journeys), no radio and an immensely long gear stick with all of three gears to choose from. Four, if you counted reverse.

Sometimes we would motor as far as Epping Forest and explore. Over time we became expert at finding our way through the thousands of acres of trees. Most visitors scarcely penetrated the timber beyond sight of their cars and we would leave these timid souls far behind. We had our own 'private' glade deep in the heart of the forest where no one else ever seemed to go and where we shared undisturbed picnic lunches.

My father was extremely playful. I am sure the games we enjoyed were as much for his benefit as for ours; he was compensating for all he had missed out on during his own childhood. Our little family of four would play rounders, French cricket, badminton (without a net, which made it slightly pointless) and, occasionally, on my mother's insistence, baseball.

That was just on outings. At home, my father instigated a nightly tradition which started when I was about three and continued until I was ten.

We called it 'The Play'. After supper, my father and I would retire to my parents' room, climb on the big double bed and try to shove each other off. Simple as that. You could use arms, legs, push, pull – whatever it took. Of course my father let me win these contests and my mother, sitting downstairs, would sigh each time another thundering crash shook the house as my father toppled to the floor of the room above.

He built me a train set, and spent far more time playing with it than I did. The little electric locomotives had funnels you could put drops in, and fake smoke would stream behind the train as it chuffed around the track. My father laid in stocks of the special chemical so that rolling stock would always look as realistic as possible when we – or he – played with it.

Bonfire night was a very big deal. As soon as fireworks were in the shops, father and son were there, carefully choosing that year's display. We considered ourselves experts and were lofty in our judgements on various brands. Standard, we decided, were most reliable, if a little dull. Brocks were livelier, but you got more duds. Astra we never touched after half of one box failed to go off. My father and I sulked for days after that. Later, whenever anything broke or failed in some way, it was described contemptuously as 'an Astra'.

Sometimes my father would drive us half a mile up the road to Crow Lane to see some real trains. The main Liverpool Street railway line ran parallel with it and we would park on top of an embankment and wait to see what my father called a 'proper' train – one pulled by a steam engine – rush past us like a snorting dragon. This was thrilling, and one day it resulted in the first great regret of my life.

One bitingly cold, snowy Saturday afternoon we saw the telltale puffs of smoke rising into the air far down the track and knew we were in luck. Soon the great black engine appeared round a distant bend and thundered towards us. I could see the fireman shovelling the coal and the driver standing on the footplate. Suddenly he noticed the tall man with two little children standing on the slope above the track and, as the distance closed, gave a huge theatrical wave.

'Come on, Richard – he's waving at us. Wave back, quickly!'

But I couldn't. It was as if a god had taken personal notice of my existence, and I froze. I could no more return this fabulous creature's wave than I could drive his train. And a moment later the chance was gone as the engine rocked past us and into a tunnel.

'What a shame . . . you won't get a chance like that again.'

I knew my father was right. I had let a wonderful opportunity to exchange waves with a train driver pass and tears of disappointment and self-recrimination sprang from my eyes. I may have been too young to understand the words '*carpe deum*' but I resolved there and then to seize my chances in future. A seminal moment. Today when I dither I tell myself: 'Remember the train driver.'

Before long the steam engines had been comprehensively replaced with electric and diesel trains and a great decade of change was under way. My mother had taught me to read and count, and one evening my father arrived home with a gleaming, freshly minted coin. 'Can you tell me what year is stamped on this, Richard?'

I studied the glittering sixpence for a few moments. 'Um . . . it's 1961.'

'Yes. Well done. You can keep it. In fact, it's time you started getting pocket money like your sister. I'll give you sixpence every week from now on, all right?'

So far then, so good. Chris was turning out to be the very model of a modern father. Putting aside what today we describe as 'quality time' for his children. Taking them out by himself once a week. Excelling in the demonstrative affection department – he was extravagant with his kisses and cuddles. I don't think a day went by when I wasn't swept into the air in a bear hug, had a huge raspberry trumpeted on my neck (unfailingly hilarious, this), or was showered with kisses at bedtime. The only occasions these offerings were muted were when we stayed at Shawbury, or if my grandparents visited us. Then a touch of formality entered the atmosphere; there was a faint air of reserve about my father and he would be less boisterous with his children. I didn't mind; it was simply part of having to 'be polite' when Grandma and Granddad were around.

On the long drives from Romford to Shawbury, my parents would inevitably discuss my grandparents and my father's upbringing. My sister and I would shamelessly eavesdrop, even to the point of demanding: 'Speak up!' or 'What was that again? I didn't catch it.' My parents were usually tolerant and would merely flash the occasional warning glance over their shoulders. 'Not a word about this at Shawbury, you two . . .'

We had no radio in our car and these conversations between my parents often lasted well over an hour. I absorbed many of Kiln Farm's secrets as I stared, unseeing, at the countryside slowly moving by. My mind's eye was busy with pictures from the past. I saw a little boy running in panic through the near-deserted farmhouse, calling for his parents. I saw the grief etched on my grandparents' faces as they buried their little boy, and Geoffrey's shock and panic when his uncle's will was read. I saw Denstone's forbidding face and the dormitories with their straw palliasses where my father had slept. I sailed with him across the Atlantic through icebergs and storms, and felt his humiliation when he was sacked before he'd even started his new job. All these things I learned on the road to Shawbury.

My father's openness and affection meant that, by the time I was about seven, I thought I'd worked out how he'd react in most situations involving me and I loved him in an uncomplicated, trusting way. But things weren't that simple. There was still a lot of unresolved damage caused by the past. Dad had done extraordinarily well in laying many of his ghosts. I wish he were alive today so I could tell him that. But he was still haunted by pernicious phantoms and they were about to make an appearance.

I think the first hint that my father might have darker dimensions to him came in 1963. I was in hospital recovering from a tonsillectomy. He had hurried over to visit me during his lunch hour, in one of his habitual charcoal suits, bringing presents and telling jokes. After he'd gone a curious nurse wandered over to my bed. 'Was that your dad, then?'

When I said yes, she made a little moue. 'He looks very strict.'

I was astonished. 'Perhaps it's his glasses,' I managed. 'Maybe that makes him look a bit strict. But he isn't at all, honestly.'

She nodded, unconvinced, and wandered off again.

I kept puzzling over her remark and, a few weeks later, believed I'd witnessed some powerful defence material to present if I ever saw her again. I saw my father cry for the first time.

The whole family had settled down in front of our black-and-white television set (we always called it a television set, not the telly or TV) to watch comedian Harry Worth's weekly show. A big treat for me – Harry came on after my bedtime but I was allowed to stay up and watch him.

The BBC continuity announcer was introducing the programme when suddenly the screen cut away to a caption that read 'Newsflash'. I was sitting on my father's lap and rocked slightly as he sat up straighter. A newsreader appeared, holding a piece of paper. The words he spoke were uttered nearly half a century ago, but I have a clear recollection of most of what he said.

'We are getting reports that President Kennedy has been shot in Dallas, Texas. The President is believed to have been wounded and has been taken to hospital. We will bring you more on this when we can.' There was a pause and then the screen faded slowly to black.

Before either of my parents could say a word, the screen brightened again and the newsreader was back, being handed a fresh piece of paper. For a few moments he looked dumbly at it, and then cleared his throat.

'I am very sorry to have to tell you ... that President Kennedy is dead.' I felt my father's entire body stiffen and my mother gave a little wail. Newscaster and nation stared blankly at each other for a few moments longer until the screen darkened again.

The trauma that swept around the world was fully represented in our small living room. My parents clung to each other in instant, overwhelming grief. My mother kept whispering: 'Oh-oh-oh-oh-oh-oh,' and my father pressed one hand to his eyes, tears dripping through his fingers. My sister and I stared at them in awe, but particularly at my father. These were the first sobs we had ever seen wrung from him.

Then bathos descended. The opening titles of *Harry Worth* were blaring out, the man himself performing his trademark sight-gag involving a reflective shop window and a porkpie hat. It was ludicrous, but Harry saved the day in homes like ours because my father managed to gasp: 'You children stay in here and watch this. Your mother and I are going into the kitchen to talk.'

Next morning my mother succumbed to a vicious migraine and had to stay in bed. My sister and I dressed in our smartest clothes and my father put on his darkest suit. We took a train into London and joined the long queue outside the American embassy, patiently waiting to sign the hastily arranged book of condolence. When it was full it would be sent to Jackie Kennedy. We seemed to shuffle slowly forward for hours in the cold November wind, but at last we were in a little anteroom and my father was handed a gold fountain pen by a man in a black coat.

Dad produced the scrap of paper on which he had drafted his message to the newly widowed woman across the Atlantic, and copied it carefully on to the page. Then we went home.

It was my first experience of the death of an icon. Seventeen years on I was old enough to understand the wave of shock and emotion that swept the world when John Lennon was shot; curiously, another seventeen years later, Princess Diana was killed. Just as with Kennedy and Lennon, millions would remember exactly where they were and what they were doing when they heard the news she was dead, and the mass grief which followed.

But at seven, I struggled to comprehend my parents' distress. They tried to explain but it made no sense. President Kennedy had never been to our house and my mother and father had not met him. Why then did they keep crying in the days after he died?

As I grew older, I came gradually to understand, and even vicariously to share, something of their emotion. Kennedy was the great post-war visionary of my parents' generation. To them, he was a hero and the antithesis to the clapped-out politics that had led to two world wars. Now I can see that my father identified with Kennedy. He wore the same style of single-breasted suit, the same narrow sober ties of silver and speckled grey, and white shirts with gleaming cuffs that always protruded a discreet inch or so beyond his jacket's sleeves. My father was not alone. For once, the glamour of the office of President was matched by the incumbent and many men wanted to be like him.

Women like my mother adored the First Lady too, and eagerly copied her fashion style. My mother was a dab hand at her Singer sewing machine and skilled at running up her own outfits. Women's magazines often gave away patterns based on Jackie's latest look and my mother would go out and buy the material. A couple of evenings later, she would sashay into our living room with a 'Well, what do you all think?' and there was Jackie Kennedy's last party frock on display in Dagenham Road.

What with my father's Kennedy-esque power suits and my mother's copied outfits, sometimes when they when out together, they looked as if they were off to a party on Capitol Hill.

Jackie not only had the same effortless grace and style as her husband, she was a mother too. Washington's press corps fell over each other to snatch photo opportunities of the young couple with their small children. The toddlers were even photographed crawling under their father's desk in the Oval Office. In the new prosperity of the 1960s, it was even possible to forgive the Kennedys their fabulous wealth.

Shortly before the assassination I remember my father calling me into the room where he was watching the evening news. Kennedy was making his historic speech about putting a man on the moon by the end of the decade. 'Did you hear what he said, Richard?' my father asked delightedly. 'He said America is going to land a man on the moon simply because they choose to do it. Imagine that. Just because they choose to. What a country!'

I have often wondered what my father would have made of JFK's prodigious womanising, had it been made public knowledge at the time. (This was a president who confided to a startled British prime minister that he suffered crippling headaches if he did not have sex at least once a day.) I think he would have moved swiftly into denial. Certainly in later years, when the subject could no longer be contained, he would brush it aside; nothing could be allowed to tarnish the burnished memory of Kennedy's Camelot.

But what really sealed the young president's hold over hearts and minds was his nerveless and adroit handling of the Cuban missile crisis. I have clear memories of this because it was the first time fear had entered our home. My parents began to disappear into the kitchen for whispered conversations, usually after the television news, and one evening I followed them.

'It might mean a general call-up, Mary, even if we get through the next few days . . .'

'That's a big if, Chris . . . but do you really think so?'

I came out from behind the door. 'What's a jenny callerp?'

My mother turned to me. 'What are you doing, Mr Spy? It's nothing. Nothing at all. Anyway, your father's too old to be called up now.'

As the Soviet/US standoff worsened, my parents tried to explain to my sister and me a little about Russians and rockets and atom bombs. It was all way above my head, but Elizabeth burst into tears and sobbed, 'Are we all going to die, then?'

Suddenly, after a week or so, the enervating atmosphere evaporated. Everyone was smiling again and saying that Mr Kennedy had saved the world.

A year later he was gunned down, and when I grew up I was increasingly puzzled that my personal memories of the day he died should be so vivid. I was only seven. Lots of people my age have no recall of it at all.

Now I believe it is because another trauma occurred almost immediately afterwards; a personal one so shocking to me that it fixed this period in my childhood in my mind for ever.

The first time my father thrashed me.

*

I suppose I must have been smacked a few times by both my parents up to this point, but I can't really remember it. I do have an image of my grandmother rapping me over the knuckles with a walking stick for saying I was 'sick of this damn weather' – swearing of any kind was not tolerated at

Kiln Farm – but it didn't really hurt, and neither was it meant to; very much a token tap.

So the shock of being beaten with a cane – a long bamboo stick, part of a big bundle kept in the garden shed for supporting runner beans in summer – was total.

I wish I could remember exactly what I did wrong that prompted the first thrashing, but that particular mental home video stubbornly refuses to roll. The tape only starts after my infraction, with my father pointing a finger at me. His hand is trembling with rage and his face is dark.

'Wait here.'

So I stand calmly in the living room, obediently waiting while he goes out into the garden. I am not particularly frightened. I am familiar with my father's occasional outbursts of temper and hearing his baritone crack as he bellows at full volume, but the worst that has ever happened is to be sent to my room for a couple of hours, or early to bed. This last punishment, involving as it does missed children's television, is certainly enough to produce tears of protest and grovelling appeals for mercy.

Today, I hear the shed door grating open. There is a stiff point where the wood tries to jam against the garden path and it always makes the same groaning rasp as it is forced open. The unmistakable sound will soon come to have a Pavlovian effect on me, producing a weakness in the knees, a spasm in the belly and a suddenly dry mouth. This first day, it's just our shed door being opened.

My father is back, holding one of the garden canes I help him plant in his vegetable patch every spring. I like to pretend the triangles and cross-lashings are wigwams, and when they are complete I lurk beneath them, waiting to ambush the Lone Ranger as he rides past. I can't imagine why he has brought one into the house.

'Turn around.'

I obey, wondering what's going on. There is a painting on the wall in front of me, of an autumnal Canadian lake with blue-grey rocks rising from the still, clear water. Perhaps I am going to have to count them, or –

The back of my legs have caught fire. I hear the dry cracking of burning wood. There it is again, and now my buttocks are burning too. Another sharp crack and my back is alight. Too shocked and consumed by agony to move at first, I find I cannot breathe either. My lungs have stopped working.

I manage to stumble into a half-turn in time to see my father bringing his stick whistling through the air in a sideways arc meant to connect with my shoulder blades, but instead it meets with the muscle of my upper arm. I collapse to my knees in agony, eyes wide, mouth open as I desperately try to suck in air.

My father steps back, breathing heavily. It occurs to me that this is why I cannot; he is using up all the air in the room.

'Right. Next time, do as you're told.'

As he walks out of the room again, I at last manage to drag in a juddering, shuddering gasp, but when I try to breathe out, a most surprising and disconcerting thing happens. I make a noise just like the whistle on our kitchen kettle when it boils.

And so I continue to kneel there awhile, screaming.

*

A new regime had begun. I quickly discerned that the beatings I was now intermittently subjected to were rarely a result of especially bad behaviour. I could tell that they stemmed from a loss of control on my father's part. He had always been prone to losing his temper and shouting at my sister and me when we were naughty, but that no longer seemed enough for him, as far as I was concerned. He did not hit Elizabeth.

I must have known that the thrashings were excessive because, tellingly, I didn't mention them to anyone. I never confided anything about it to anyone at Rush Green Junior School, which I walked to each morning. I realised after several playground conversations about parental discipline that although many of my friends were also physically chastised, my own beatings were of a different order. The ultimate sanction in other homes seemed to be a ritual whack across the palm with a ruler or belt, or the application of a slipper to the bottom. One boy said his father kept a stick in a cupboard and would occasionally brandish it in heated moments, but had never actually struck any of his children with it.

I cannot remember how frequent the thrashings were. They must have been staggered because I can distinctly recall periods where I decided they must have stopped for good. Then I would do something to enrage my father and my heart would falter as once again I stood alone in a room, listening to the distant shed door grind open.

My mother was torn. She had sworn to love, honour and obey her husband and he had a dominant 'I know best' attitude to disciplining his son. I don't think she was fully aware how hard I was being hit; I have a dim memory of my father downplaying it in a row with her about it.

When I discussed it with her recently, she told me that the issue became an increasingly serious one in her marriage. She was very unhappy about the situation, but the canings usually took place when she was not in the house – often on a Saturday – and, for some reason I still don't fully understand, I didn't tell her what had happened when she arrived home. I think that, at a fundamental level, I felt ashamed of myself. And as my father didn't actually draw blood or break bones, I just wanted to forget the experiences as quickly as possible and pushed them to the back of my mind. It was some time before matters came to a head.

And, of course, corporal punishment in schools was de rigueur in the 1960s. Later I would be caned several times at my grammar school – for the most trivial of reasons; I once received three strokes for throwing a paper dart in an English class – and got short shrift from my parents when I informed them. Until recently, troublesome youths were routinely birched by order of the magistrates; the culture was quite astonishingly different just a few decades ago.

Because my father continued being a loving, indulgent parent in the sunny periods between the beatings, I was confused. As quickly as an hour after a caning he would be speaking gently to me and even offering contrite apologies.

I also think I dimly discerned that these rages, so painful for me when they erupted, had little or nothing to do with my behaviour. I knew the punishments were completely disproportionate to the crimes. And today, I am certain they were the last reflex stirrings of the abiding resentment my father felt about his own childhood. I was quite literally his whipping boy, for a time. His anger went very deep and occasionally it would consume him completely. That doesn't justify what he did to me over a two or three year period, but I have to reconcile his basic decency and gentleness as a father with these grotesque outpourings of violent anger.

Significantly, he never struck my sister, let alone my mother. It was a strictly father–son thing.

*

I was nearly ten and had bumped into my mother at the shops as I walked home from school. I persuaded her to buy a packet of Rolos for us all to share after supper that evening.

Back home watching *Blue Peter*, I called to her in the kitchen.

'Mum, can I have one of those Rolos?'

'No. After supper.'

'Go on. Just one . . .'

'Oh, all right. They're in my raincoat pocket. Just one, though.'

'Promise.'

Fifteen minutes later, as Valerie Singleton told us the programme's cat was getting over the flu, I was looking in horror at the ripped paper on the carpet in front of me. There was just one Rolo left.

I stuffed it back into my mother's pocket with the wrappings and hoped for the best. Maybe I could blame it on Elizabeth.

Later, after we'd all eaten, my mother went to get the sweets. She came back with the solitary survivor, looking more amused than cross.

'OK, who ate all of these?'

My sister had only arrived home a couple of minutes before the meal so I couldn't pin it on her. I was about to confess when I glanced at my father. His face had gone the sinister shade of dark red I knew so well, and I panicked.

'Not me. Honestly, Mum . . . Dad. Not me.'

'Come on, Richard, it couldn't have been anyone el–'

But my father interrupted her.

'I will not have you lying. I will not have it. You get one more chance. Did you eat all of them?'

I thought of the one remaining chocolate.

'Well . . . not exactly. I left –'

'Go to your room and wait.'

My mother grimaced. 'Chris, no. It's only a few sweets, for heaven's sake. We can . . .'

But her husband had already left the room. I walked silently up the stairs and waited in my bedroom, listening to the grinding of the shed door and trying to breathe normally.

My father came in with the cane.

'Wait, Dad, I was only –'

'Take off your shirt.'

'What?'

'Now.'

This was new. I reluctantly pulled it over my head and at once the beating began. But after the first agonising strokes, delivered randomly across my chest and waist, something deep inside me revolted. I rushed at my father, kicking and punching him and trying to grab the bamboo. He thrust me off easily and a bizarre chase ensued, with me hopping round the room and over my bed, the cane whistling through the air behind me and occasionally making stinging contact.

Finally my father – not the fittest of men – gave up, completely out of breath. He hurled his stick at me and stormed out. I threw it back at him and collapsed on my bed, shocked and in tremendous pain.

The noise of the encounter must have filled the house. As did the colossal row which now took place between my parents. Elizabeth crept into my room. 'Mum says she's going to call the police.'

The row stopped suddenly and a few moments later my mother appeared in front of me.

'Put the light on, darling. I want to look at you.'

I realised I had been sitting in the growing dark and switched on my bedside lamp, its shade askew after the exciting events of a few minutes before.

My mother stared at my upper body.

'It's all right. It's all going to be all right. I'll just go and fetch some Green Ointment from the bathroom. Stay there.'

Green Ointment was the Savlon of its day and our family swore by it. My mother came back and dabbed it along the multiple weals on my arms and body, and on the fingers that had been bruised trying to snatch away my father's stick.

'Wait here, my love. I'll be back with some hot chocolate in a minute.'

She went back downstairs again and this time the only

voice I could hear was hers, a low, endless monotone which for some reason my father did not interrupt. I fell asleep before the hot chocolate arrived.

*

Next morning was a Friday: PE day for my class. There was no question of my being allowed to go to school. Although none of my injuries were serious, the marks left by the bamboo were livid and there could be no explaining them away. The police would be informed.

My father was silent at breakfast. My mother did the talking.

'Your father is extremely ashamed of himself. He will be apologising to you later, but I am going to tell you something first. He has promised me faithfully never to hit you again. He knows what will happen if he breaks this promise. I don't believe he will, otherwise we wouldn't all be sitting here now.'

My father cleared his throat and looked at me for the first time. 'I have to go to Shrewsbury this morning, to pick up an American car. It's one of the new Ford Mustangs. The company are lending it to Prince Philip. I thought I'd stop off at Shawbury on the way. Would you like to come?'

An hour later we were belting up the M1 in a green-striped Lotus Cortina. It seemed as if my father's total loss of control the night before had shriven his soul because without moving his eyes from the road ahead he began to make the humblest apology I have ever been offered. I instinctively believed he was truly sincere, not just in his anguished regrets, but also in his passionate promises never to hit me again.

I was right to trust my judgement. He never beat me again, or threatened to. As we swept towards Kiln Farm, my father tried to explain how he thought his rages were something to do with his boyhood. He wasn't making excuses, he said, there were none to make. And after the apologies and promises, his conversation increasingly became more with himself than with me. I was not yet ten, but I detected, for the first time, the childhood source of his sporadic rages. It was an explanation that made sense even then, long before I traced the thread of betrayal and rejection running between the generations that preceded me.

Looking back after all these years, I see my father's violent outbreaks towards me as a kind of descent into madness. Other children have it harder; there are far worse forms of abuse than being caned. Thanks to my mother's stand and his own nascent if belated insight, my father finally fixed the last part of him broken by his childhood. I long ago forgave him my involuntary part in the process.

And I got to ride back to London in a Mustang.

*

Even though I was still only nine, I could tell that my father's apology was sincere. I was in no doubt he was frightened. I took what my mother had said the morning after the final thrashing as an implicit threat to go to the police, and a few years ago she confirmed to me that was exactly what she meant. She had been explicit about that in private with my father, also telling him she would leave him on the spot if he ever took a cane to me again, and bring my sister and me with her.

But most of all, he was ashamed. He had lost control and belatedly been forced to confront his behaviour, and how grotesquely disproportionate his punishment was to my 'crime'. He was also reflecting on the violent retributions he had taken on me over recent years and those weighed heavily on his conscience too. All this he later confessed to my mother.

As we sped south in the red and cream Mustang, attracting startled looks from other drivers all the way back down the motorway, I instinctively trusted my father's promise that he would never beat me again. I put my faith in him, as sons do when their fathers make solemn vows to them. And as time went by and the cane remained absent from its cobwebbed corner in our garden shed, I realised an unpleasant chapter had definitely closed. The bond of trust between my father and me was restored, never to be breached again.

I sometimes wonder if I have over-sentimentalised this episode, been too quick to write off the debt my father incurred. These were, after all, a series of savage assaults on a child for which he was never brought to book or punished. But the reason I forgave him then – and now – is, I think, because the contrition he displayed was without artifice. Children know when they are being emotionally manipulated, even if they are powerless to do anything about it. My father was truly humbled by the realisation of what he had done. I could see that. And perhaps my automatic act of forgiveness transferred a degree of power and control from father to son.

I don't think this unpleasant interlude in my childhood had any particularly lasting effect on me. I don't wince when I pass a bamboo trellis, I don't have bad dreams in which I am being beaten. I harbour no dark fantasy of swishing a cane myself. Children are adaptable creatures and live in the present. I dealt with the thrashings as best I could while they were happening and, when they stopped, mostly forgot about them.

And now there was a considerable distraction from the receding unpleasantness. It was 1966 and England was hosting the World Cup. Excitement at Dagenham Road was intense. My bedroom began to fill with World Cup paraphernalia: posters of the star players; collections of swap-cards featuring the entire home team; and sundry incarnations of the tournament's mascot, a cheerful stubby cartoon lion called World Cup Willie.

There were only two television channels then – BBC and ITV – and both had their own listings magazines, which scorned to mention their rival's programmes. So, like most households, we took copies of both: the BBC's *Radio Times* and the commercial channel's brasher version, *TV Times*. As the first international clashes neared, both magazines became heavily dog-eared and annotated – largely by my mother, who left reminders for herself in the margins.

'England v France. Beef casserole. Prepare in afternoon and serve at half-time.' Or: 'England v Portugal. Sandwiches before kick-off, soup and rolls at full-time. If extra time, Shredded Wheat for Chris.'

My father and I hosted daily conferences at the breakfast table to discuss England's prospects, during which my mother and sister were generously allowed to listen, and even to make the occasional contribution. My father knew the England striker Jimmy Greaves very slightly, through a business connection with Ford, and we talked about the Spurs player as if he was an old family friend. Jimmy would do this, Jimmy would almost certainly not do that, and so on.

Jimmy actually did nothing much at all and, after an early injury, was dropped by the coach, Alf Ramsay. The Madeleys were unimpressed with their man's replacement, a toothy West Ham player called Geoff Hurst. We doubted he could fill our hero's boots.

The tournament progressed and so did England. My father and I were quite certain victory would be ours, and tried to mask the heavy burden of responsibility we carried, when in front of the womenfolk.

Actually we knew virtually nothing at all about football and much of our early morning discussions about tactics came straight from the back pages of the *Daily Express*. One morning I quietly assured my sister that she need have nothing to fear from that night's game with Portugal and their dangerously talented goal-scorer Eusebio. England's celebrated defender, the toothless Nobby Stiles, would 'tuck Eusebio up'.

'What do you mean, tuck him up?' she asked.

I had no idea. 'Er . . . you know, tuck him up. A bit like when you make an apple-pie bed, sort of thing.'

'What, so he can't move and falls over?'

'Um, something like that, yes . . . er . . . don't worry, Liz. You'll see tonight.'

I quickly changed the subject.

As my father and I had predicted all along, England made it to the final against West Germany. Unashamed xenophobia reigned.

'If we managed to beat Hitler, we can beat that shower,' my father told me, shaving on the morning of the big game.

As it was just the two of us, I allowed my doubts to show.

'Yes,' I said uncertainly, 'but they've got to the final, haven't they? They must be pretty good. Anyway, surely most of them weren't born until after the war?'

My father snorted and flecks of shaving foam speckled the mirror.

'Only up to a point, only up to a point. Anyway, you never hear them talking about what their fathers did during the war, do you, eh? But we'll beat the Jerries all right, don't you worry. They're obsessed with efficiency, the Germans; can't think on their feet like us. Look at Dunkirk . . .'

And we did. The final whistle blew and we all yelled ourselves hoarse. My father and I shook hands in mutual congratulation. Naturally, we modestly forbore to claim credit for our victory. But we knew what we had achieved.

I raced to the front door and opened it, half-expecting to see cheering crowds and impromptu street parties. Dagenham Road looked as if a neutron bomb had been dropped. There was no sign of human life, no cars or buses, cyclists or pedestrians. Everyone was locked in joyous communion with their television sets. I rushed back to ours and there was Nobby Stiles, prancing around with the lid of the trophy on his head like a schoolboy's cap. He'd tucked everyone up, all right.

Years later, Judy and I interviewed a man who had suffered

a serious head injury in 1965. He lay in a coma for a quarter of a century and then surprised doctors by slowly regaining consciousness. He knew nothing of the world since the accident, and his wife, who had stood by him all that time, was doing her best to fill him in on what he'd missed – the end of the Cold War, computers, the Falklands War, that sort of thing. It was, she told us somewhat wearily during the conversation with them both, an uphill task.

A light went on in my head.

'Have you told him about what happened in the 1966 World Cup?' I asked her.

She turned to her husband. 'Have I, dear?'

He thought for a moment. 'I don't think so. I remember that we qualified . . .' He looked at me. 'How did we do?'

I savoured the moment and then said, 'We won.'

He burst out laughing.

'No, seriously – how far did we get?'

'Honestly – we won. We beat West Germany 4–2 in extra time. Geoff Hurst scored a hat-trick.'

I can still see the look on his face. He must have been the last man in England to get the news.

I was ten that same year. My parents threw me a birthday party to celebrate their son reaching double figures. About a dozen friends – all boys – came, and things quickly descended into anarchy. My father had insisted on personally organising a treasure hunt. Ten objects had to be found, and the first team back to base won a prize – a crisp green one-pound note, improbably wrapped in silver foil.

It says much about the more trusting mood of those days that the treasure hunt involved boys pairing off in hunting packs of two and being encouraged to roam the district unsupervised, in search of discarded bus tickets with specific serial numbers, branded paper bags from certain shops, pond weed from the deep gravel pits half a mile away, and other bric-a-brac. All this involved crossing busy main roads and taking buses to Romford town centre and back again. Lots of my friends were still only nine, but it was taken for granted that they were perfectly competent to do this, and would be quite safe.

Hard to imagine today.

In the event, almost everyone arrived back simultaneously at the house with their nine pieces of treasure. We were handed the envelopes containing the tenth and final demand, couched in rhyme, like all the others.

> Now comes the Holy Grail
> Your final journey on this trail.
> Thus you must go searching for
> Not hay – but proper yellow straw.

This was a serious miscalculation on my father's part. After a moment's collective thought, a great shout went up.

'The rabbit!' There was a stampede down to the bottom of the garden and the hutch where my sister's black and white Dutch bunny, Flopsy, lived. The wood-and-wire door was torn open and half a dozen grimy hands groped inside for the straw on which Flopsy usually dozed, but now lay quivering in terror. After a few seconds of grunting, panting and fighting, everyone thundered back to the house. Behind them,

Flopsy lay on his back, eyes staring, unseeing, towards the ceiling of his little home. Elizabeth, who had followed the raiding party down the path shouting, 'No, no, stop', pulled her pet out from the ruin of his home. Flopsy had died, instantly, from shock.

My best mate Nigel Woods pocketed the prize anyway and everyone went home, a bit subdued, but not that much. It had been a great party.

After we'd waved the last of them goodbye, Elizabeth and my mother turned on my father, and I crept out of the house until things had calmed down.

Flopsy was interred under the pear tree.

*

Meanwhile I was growing up. Rush Green Junior gave way to grammar school – Coopers Company, on Tredegar Square just off the Mile End Road in Bow. It was a ghastly place, living on its past reputation as a guild school established by the Worshipful Company of Coopers in the mid-1500s. By the time I got there in the second half of the twentieth century, Coopers was a bizarre battleground; a freakish blend of public school-style tradition and modern yobbery. Staff were baffled and intimidated by the gangs of skinheads who dominated the classrooms. Discipline was in tatters. Most of the boys were from the East End – I was one of a small contingent who commuted in from the suburbs. Our 'posh' accents – Ha! Essex boys, we! – marked us as outsiders. One by one we were picked off. I kept a low profile longer than most, partly because I was in the school rugby team. But once the other pariahs had fled in terror to schools back in their native suburbia, my turn came.

Coopers had a knife culture long before the current street vogue for carrying blades. One day when I was fourteen one of my few remaining friends whispered that I was going to be 'rumbled' – cut – on my way to Mile End Tube station after school. I knew he was unlikely to be joking; things were getting increasingly out of hand. One boy had been beaten unconscious outside the school gates with a metal chair leg; another had been shot point-blank in the mouth with a .22 air pistol.

Staff were in denial about the steady rise in violence at Coopers. When I went to the headmaster's office to put myself under his protection, he dismissed me out of hand. The choice lay between having a verbal confrontation with him, or a metallic one with his pupils and an exciting trip by ambulance to Whitechapel Hospital. I chose the argument. I insisted on phoning my father at Ford's head office in Brentwood.

Like most schoolboys, I had kept the fact I was being bullied to myself. I didn't see what my parents could do about it. In any case, like most adolescents intimidated by their peer group, I felt as ashamed as I did frightened.

My father must have been surprised to get a call out of the blue from his son informing him that a casual stabbing was in the offing. But he was urbane.

'Well, we can't have you coming home with puncture wounds,' he said reasonably. 'Put me on to the head, will you?'

Their conversation was brief and mostly conducted at the other end. The headmaster replaced the receiver with a curt: 'Your father will collect you in an hour. You are to remain in my office until then.'

Dad arrived soon after school finished for the day and as we drove past Tredegar Square's scruffy park, we spotted my persecutors lurking in the bushes. My father grunted. 'That's your last day at Coopers. You won't be seeing that lot again.'

'Isn't that . . . a bit cowardly?'

He glanced at me. 'Don't be idiotic. Even at Denstone I never thought I was going to be stabbed.'

You could say I left Coopers at knifepoint, but I would probably have changed schools anyway. We had recently moved out of Greater London to rural Essex. It was a long haul every day in and out of the East End, although I could do most of my homework on the train.

I transferred to Shenfield Tech, soon to become one of the first of the new comprehensives. Shenfield was a 'mixed' school – what we now call co-ed – so, for the first time in three years, I was in the same class as girls. Teenage girls. I was completely tongue-tied with them and for months barely spoke a word to the lithe beauties who eyed me coolly across the classroom.

But if a strong female presence raised the adolescent sexual temperature, it had the opposite effect on the boys' tendency to belligerence. The atmosphere was far calmer and friendlier than at Coopers and bullying was rare, largely because the girls loudly denounced it if they spotted it. For me, knives and air pistols in the playground were things of the past.

Brentwood – a corruption of the medieval 'Burnt Wood', so named after a long-forgotten inferno – was once part of a great forest that covered much of Essex. An expanse of timber to the northwest at Epping is the largest surviving chunk, but Hartswood, on the southern edge of Brentwood, is pretty big too. My parents had had an eye on the spot ever since Ford moved their HQ to the area from its massive factory in nearby Dagenham. So when a semi went on the market they snapped it up.

The Madeleys' vista from their front door in Romford had included a launderette, a tobacconist's and a bus stop. Our new home looked out on a dense wall of trees standing immediately opposite on the other side of the street. Only a few more houses continued along our side of the road before it was swallowed up by thick woodland on either side. A mile or so distant lay fields and ancient parkland. My hunger for the countryside, an appetite sharpened by so many holidays to Shawbury, was at last satisfied.

In the months after we moved to Brentwood, before I fled Coopers, I would press my nose against the carriage window as my train rattled in or out of the station, staring at the ploughed fields and spinneys that narrowly – but definitely, satisfyingly – separated the town from what William Cobbett described as 'the great wen' – London's sprawl. The sense of living in a small town surrounded by a moat of greenery – a narrow band of greenery, admittedly, towards the capital, but broad and expansive on the other side looking towards Suffolk and Hertfordshire – held great importance for me. I was now able to pretend to myself that we 'lived in the country', a concept few in Brentwood even thirty-five years ago would have shared. It is only today, looking back on my early adolescence, that I realise how deeply so many visits to Kiln Farm had affected me. I so longed for its fields and hedgerows, copses and streams, that I tried to replicate it wherever possible.

When I was thirteen my father, nagged incessantly by my grandfather, gave me an air rifle for Christmas.

'The boy must learn how to shoot,' Geoffrey had insisted. 'When he comes to Shawbury he can help me keep the vermin down.' By vermin he meant the wood pigeons that raided his cornfields and winter greens, the rabbits that caused havoc in his wife's vegetable garden, and the grey squirrels that robbed him of almost all the hazelnuts the brakes in his orchard produced every autumn.

My mother hated my air gun and there was a matriarchal no-shooting decree back home. But with what to me seemed a limitless forest on my doorstep, I couldn't resist temptation and secretly crept across the road on many dawns to practise my shooting skills. Two brothers who lived next door had air guns too and we usually went together. We were never caught; our parents slept on, oblivious, and the wood was empty at such an early hour. After filtering a few yards through the trees, we had entered another world.

But increasingly we left our rifles behind. We were falling under the spell of a great English deciduous forest.

In winter, Hartswood was pungent with the scent of decaying leaves, moss and wilting bracken. We might pick up the unmistakable rank scent of a fox and track him to his earth.

Badger setts were harder to find but when snow fell it was easier to follow their spoor home, a dugout usually hidden under an old tree root in a clay bank. We marked where the animals slept and when spring and summer came spent hours watching their young playing. Sunset was the best time to see the fox cubs; you needed at least a half-moon to see badgers. I loved these expeditions. Most of all, I looked forward to describing them to my grandfather on my next visit to Shawbury.

He always listened with grave attention, followed by precise questions and, finally, his advice on woodcraft.

'If you hear jays starting to scream in the distance – you know jays are members of the crow, family, don't you, Richard? Yes, of course you do – well, jays are the forest watchdogs. If they start to make a fuss, they've like as not seen a fox moving under the trees. Stay still and you'll probably see him too, as long as you're downwind of him. That's another thing, Richard – always enter the wood with the wind against you. Your scent won't carry ahead to the wild things . . . you'll see much more that way.'

For my fourteenth birthday, Granddad gave me *The Book of British Birds*, inscribed, 'To my fellow bird-watcher'. His present didn't embarrass me in the slightest, something which surprises me a little now. After all, I had recently moved to a co-ed school and was busy discovering girls. It was 1970 and I was increasingly immersed in the rock and pop culture; I was into Yes, Free, Al Stewart and Cream. I was growing my hair long – to my father's utter consternation – and learning to play guitar under the instruction of a teacher who had once accompanied Paul

Simon on stage. I was even part of a rudimentary folk-rock band, called, appallingly, 'Alchemy'. Our high point would be to play a set at the 1974 Windsor Pop Festival.

Yet I was secretly delighted to be described by my grand-father as a 'bird-watcher'. I emphasise the word 'secretly' – this was not a soubriquet I could possibly share with friends. But I cherished the bond that was forming between us and I basked in the old man's approval. I took *The Book of British Birds* to bed with me most nights and studied it carefully, par-ticularly the section on species that lived on farmland. Once, in an earnest discussion with Granddad about the prolific reproduction cycle of the hated wood pigeon, he smiled and nodded at me. 'Quite the expert ornithologist, eh?'

Today, I understand the dynamic that was shaping my emerging friendship with Geoffrey. We had discovered common ground. Until this point ours was a polite but per-functory relationship. Now the fourteen-year-old boy and seventy-year-old man had found a common interest. We may have been discussing jays or pigeons or green woodpeckers; what we were really doing was developing shared language. We could just as well have been discussing football; it was the form of our conversations, not the content, that really mat-tered. We had become friends and delighted in each other's company on our long walks through Kiln Farm's fields and spinneys, or sitting on the banks of the Roden waiting for the fish to rise on summer evenings.

Geoffrey had plenty of time to spare for such moments. A few years earlier, soon after he turned sixty, he had been poleaxed by a near-fatal heart attack. Years of smoking untipped Player's had narrowed his arteries to wormholes and one night, after he had gone to bed, his heart contorted and twisted in furious attempts to expel a treacherous blood clot. It was touch and go; the doctor who came to him in the night told Kitty to expect the worst by morning.

But Geoffrey's life force was strong. He recovered. In later years, cancer came to take him, and was denied in its turn.

His destiny was to survive, intact, into old age. He could not slip away. Not quite yet.

*

After Geoffrey's coronary, my Uncle Jim ran Kiln Farm.

It left my grandfather with a lot of time on his hands. He went on long walks around Shawbury – doctor's orders – and my mother often joined him. It was on these long rambles that he began increasingly to confide in her. He told her how he had felt when he realised his family had gone to Canada without him; about the girl he fell in love with there years later; about William's betrayal. He even spoke something of John, and the pain of losing his little boy. But not much about this: the subject of John remained deeply painful territory.

Classical music became an even greater comfort to him than before. My father bought him a modern hi-fi unit, replacing the ancient reel-to-reel tape recorder and gramophone he had used since the 1950s, and the two of them listened to classical music together, eyes closed, lost in the discourse of the great composers.

Of course, stereo sound was no use to my grandfather. He

had been deaf in one ear since the trenches and could only hear in mono.

Once, I watched them sitting side by side in armchairs pushed together in the middle of the room, with speakers on either side, and heard my grandfather ask, 'Where's the soloist, Chris?'

His son pointed to a corner. 'Over there.'

My grandfather nodded. 'Extraordinary.'

It was the way they were able to communicate emotionally. Timeless music had become an alternative language they appreciated together. After one long session, they slowly opened their eyes and shyly nodded and smiled at one another. They understood what the other had felt. It was a touching moment to witness.

By now I was sixteen and clear on what I wanted to do. Go to university to study English, and then get a graduate trainee placement on some newspaper. I was going to be a reporter, like my dad. Earlier dreams about becoming a fighter pilot had blurred and faded along with my eyesight; you needed 20/20 vision to fly supersonic jets – the only things I wanted to fly – and the slight myopia and astigmatism that materialised when I was thirteen grounded that ambition for good.

But everything I read and heard about journalism sounded fun. Even my father's starving days in Canada had a touch of glamour about them, I thought, and anyway times had changed. Newspapers were thriving and local radio and regional television news were flourishing too.

In June 1972 I sat my final O level – the GCSE of the day – and dashed off a letter to my local paper. I suggested to the editor of the *Brentwood Argus* that he let me spend a few weeks in his newsroom, making tea, fetching and carrying generally, and getting a flavour of life on a weekly title.

The reply was curt. His reporters were far too busy news-gathering to keep an eye on some sixteen-year-old lad and anyway they made their own tea, thanks. I could come in for a quick chat about the business on a slack day if I liked, though.

I secretly admired the brusqueness. This was what news-paper people were famed for, wasn't it? My father coached me on what questions to ask and a few days later I sat in the editor's office, surrounded by inky proofs, newsroom rotas and expense claims that lay in a tray marked 'Abandon all hope ye who enter here'. Every single person I glimpsed in the newsroom next door was smoking furiously and hammering away on ancient Underwood typewriters.

I had never felt more at home.

I can't recall much about the interview but I do remember how it ended. The editor – a Dorset man called Brian Davies who I learned later had once hurled a pitchfork at a German Messerschmitt as it thundered low over his parents' farm during the Battle of Britain – eyed me up speculatively before saying, in his West Country accent, 'I've got a cub reporter's job going. Was going to advertise. Yours if you want it. Three-year apprenticeship. We call 'em indentures. Start tomorrow. Pay's rubbish, but you can fiddle your expenses a bit. What do you say?'

I said I needed to discuss it with my parents and tottered out on to the street. The editor's sash window on the first floor above slid up with a crash and his head appeared. 'Need to know by ten tomorrow.' He vanished again.

I called my father when I got home and he immediately left his office for a crash summit at Hartswood Road.

'Well, what do you think, Dad? It means not going to university, not even going back to school to do A levels . . .'

'Your mother thinks it's completely bonkers.'

'I know, she already said. What do *you* think?'

My father sighed and removed his glasses, rubbing his eyes.

'To be absolutely honest, I have no fucking idea.'

It was the first time I had ever heard him use the F-word. I was speechless.

He jammed his specs back and reached for the phone. 'But I know some people that probably do. Give me a couple of hours.'

For most of that evening my father rang round his contacts in the press. Some were friends from the old post-war days, others were journalists and columnists he'd got to know through the Ford press office. To a man – and the occasional woman (it was the early 1970s) – they said I should grab this unexpected opportunity with both hands. If all went well I would be years ahead of the game when my contemporaries – and potential career rivals – were still waiting to hear if they'd got their degrees.

There was only one caveat. 'He *is* sure this is what he wants to do, isn't he, Chris? Otherwise he'd better just go back to school.'

'*Are* you sure?'

I looked at my father, bleary-eyed and husky-voiced from

hours on the phone, most of a pack of Piccadilly filter tips screwed into a pile of butt-ends in the ashtray on our hall table.

'Yes. I think so. Would . . . would you have been?'

'I think so. Yes. Absolutely.'

'Mum's going to hate this.'

'I'll talk to her.'

I stole a beer from the fridge and took it to bed. As I drifted off to sleep I heard my parents talking in their room down the hall, and went to use our shared bathroom so I could listen in.

'I suppose you're right,' my mother was saying. 'I just wish he'd never gone to see the bloody man so we didn't have to decide.'

My father coughed and the light coming from under their bedroom door snapped out.

'Me too.' There was silence, and I was almost back in my room when I heard Dad say sleepily, 'Well, sod it, anyway. If it's all a ghastly mistake he can always take his A levels at evening classes, can't he?'

*

I loved being a reporter. Any lingering doubts over leaving school at sixteen evaporated in the excitement of learning my trade. There is no doubt I romantically identified with my father as a young man. I was too young to drive a car but I could legally ride a moped, and the puny 50cc Honda I bought with my first wages – eleven pounds forty pence a week – was, to my mind, the roaring Norton of my father's youth. The fact that I was doing exactly the same job he had done made me feel extraordinarily grown-up.

I told him the stories of my days when I arrived home whether he wanted to hear them or not and this, I failed to realise in my coltish enthusiasm, became increasingly wearing. In fact, when I think back to my incessant chatter at the end of what was after all a working day for him, I grow warm with latent embarrassment. He did his best to hide his mounting irritation at my callow youthfulness, but by the time I was eighteen there was much tension between us, and the atmosphere in the house was increasingly charged. One evening I bounced, Tigger-like, from the room after a bad-tempered exchange about the best way to cover a breaking story and a few minutes later I overheard my father telling my mother, 'Honestly, Mary, I'll be glad when he gets a place of his own. I know he doesn't mean to, but he's driving me nuts.'

Too much testosterone under one roof. By chance, I was about to transfer to the biggest newspaper in our group, the *East London Advertiser*, so I arranged to rent a room in a friend's house in Leytonstone. I can still see the look of suppressed relief on my father's face when I gave him the news.

It was the beginning of a long, and ultimately final, separation from my father. Not emotionally – within weeks of my moving out the claustrophobic ill temper between us vanished – but I was not a particularly dutiful son in the period that followed. Visits home became fewer and fewer as I pursued my career. By the time I was nineteen, I was News Editor on the *Advertiser*; then Assistant Editor. I was a young man in a hurry; I secretly fretted that perhaps I should have stayed at school and gone to university after all. So I made every moment, every opportunity, count.

I was still only nineteen when I decided I should move into broadcasting. A couple of years earlier, I had gone with my father to watch an edition of *The Money Programme* go out live on BBC2. The subject matter was stodgy enough – a profile of Ford – but the atmosphere surrounding the transmission of a live networked programme was a revelation to me. It was electrifying. We stood in the director's gallery where a dozen monitors flickered and a girl counted time on interviews which had to run to the second. The director called his camera shots and the producer bit his nails with tension while on the studio floor the presenter stayed cool and laid back. But, just a few feet behind the cameras, you could have squeezed the adrenalin out of the air.

After the programme, my father and I went out for dinner with the host, Brian Widlake, to a French restaurant in Shepherd's Bush. It was the first foreign restaurant I had ever eaten in and I felt grown-up and sophisticated. The young production team joined us. They were confident and cool and sexy and I wanted to be like them.

On the last train home from Liverpool Street, my father said, 'It's too late for me, but if I were you I'd be hoping to get into television. That's where the fun is. Boy, wasn't that *great*?'

Now I was applying to join the local radio stations that were starting to mushroom across the country. Most of them rejected me with a variation on the same theme.

'Sorry, son. Too young.'

I persisted. Finally I was given an interview at BBC Radio

Carlisle, 350 miles north. Somehow I talked my way into a job there as a reporter and in May 1976 found myself hammering up the M6 to start a one-year contract.

My father professed himself delighted. 'BBC, Richard – gilt-edged. You're on your way.'

Secretly, I now know, he was sinking into a strange depression. I might as well have emigrated to Australia as far as he was concerned. He told my mother, 'We'll hardly ever see him now. We hardly ever saw him after he moved out and he was only six miles down the road. It's my fault; I drove him away with my grouchiness. He heard me saying I wished he'd leave me that time. Perhaps I'll never see him again.'

My mother told him he was talking melodramatic twaddle, and so would I had I known the direction his thoughts were leading. But he didn't speak to me about it.

Now, his conviction that we would somehow lose touch with each other has a slightly sinister aspect to it, in the light of subsequent events.

I wonder if he had a premonition.

Chapter 9

———

LEFT BEHIND

The Ford was slewed diagonally across the front drive where he'd left it. Even though it was close to midnight when I pulled up outside the house where my father had died nearly twelve hours earlier, a sense of urgency and drama lingered over the spot; the same unmistakable atmosphere generated by the breaking news events I had experienced a hundred times before, covering other people's stories.

The driver's door was still wide open, office papers spilling out from the foot well and on to the drive. All the courtesy lights in the car were burning, but with a yellow tinge. The battery was running flat.

The front door of number 53 was open too, but no sound emerged, no sobbing or anguished conversation; just a thick fog of silence. My wife of nine days and I stared at each other, drained after the 150-mile non-stop drive back from our honeymoon in the West Country.

I looked inside the car. It was in wild disorder, a complete contrast to my father's usual neatness. The floor-mat on the driver's side was scrunched up and wedged tight under the foot pedals; I could only think it had jammed there as he kicked out in a reflex response to the agonising pains in his chest. Business papers and memos were strewn everywhere; I had no idea why. It couldn't have been the work of a passing thief because my father's wallet lay on the passenger seat, banknotes untouched inside.

The gear stick was still in first. The handbrake had been pulled up with such force that later I had a hard job releasing it.

I sat in his seat for a while, picturing how it must have been. Then, for the first time, I wept for my dead father.

*

My first marriage was a mistake mostly of my own making. I rushed into it and no one tried to stop me, least of all my parents. Lynda was the girl in the flat below mine. I moved into the shared house a few weeks after arriving in Carlisle; I was settling in at the radio station all right but, God, I was lonely. My new colleagues were nothing like the young newspaper journalists I had left behind in London. BBC local radio was pretty stuffy back then and Radio Carlisle was run like an outpost of Radio Four. Everyone was much older than me – I was still only nineteen – and from completely different professional backgrounds. They were kind and welcoming but socially we had nothing in common.

Most evenings after work I'd either sit alone in a pub with a pint and a paper, or watch TV in my bedsit. For the first time in my life I was experiencing homesickness. It made me wonder how on earth my father had managed when he arrived in a strange city in a strange country, so much further from home than I was. Carlisle was hardly Canada; I could always belt back down the motorway for the weekend. Nevertheless, I began to think I'd made a bad mistake. Then I met Lynda, a pretty, feisty girl who ran a boutique in the little city. She was confident, a few years older than me, and we hit it off straight away.

Within what seemed like five minutes I had asked her to marry me. It was a classic folie à deux; I should never have asked her and she should never have said yes, but somehow we found ourselves setting up home together in a rented bungalow miles from anywhere at the foot of the Caldbeck fells. A few months later we were walking up the aisle of a tiny country Cumbrian church in the next village. She was twenty-eight and I barely twenty-one. Our astonished parents were the only witnesses.

As a cure for my loneliness, it worked. As a marriage, it didn't. Looking back, I can hardly believe I was so reckless with two lives and for a long time I couldn't understand why my parents hadn't counselled their boy to show more caution. During my brief engagement I could tell they had misgivings they tried to conceal. Five years later, after my divorce, I decided it was time to ask my mother what they had really thought about my whirlwind wedding.

'Obviously we could see you were rushing into things,' she

said, 'but we couldn't understand why. You never told us then how lonely you were, just like you didn't let on about the bullying at school. I suppose we thought the two of you were on a great romantic adventure. So we didn't say anything.'

'I bloody well wish you had, Mum. It might have made me stop and think. Anyway, why couldn't you?'

'It was your father. He wouldn't allow it. I've told you before how worried he was that he was going to lose touch with you. I kept telling him that was nonsense but he just couldn't get it out of his head. He thought if he warned you against marrying in haste you'd . . . oh, I don't know, you'd react badly, withdraw from him. You always were your own person. He figured you'd get married anyway, and resent him for trying to stop you. Then if it didn't work out, you'd resent the fact he *hadn't* stopped you.'

I was astonished. I couldn't understand how my father had managed to think himself into such a tortured position. He seems to have succumbed to a kind of superstitious inertia. It was totally out of character for him to be paralysed by what amounted to sheer second-guessing.

He'd given me plenty of unasked-for advice in the past and I'd never taken it amiss. I'd never taken it much either, whether he was advising me to get a haircut – 'You're a reporter. You have to look smart at all times. You never know who you'll suddenly have to interview' – or berating my choice of car. 'Why don't you get yourself a Ford? You look ridiculous in that foreign thing you've got yourself.' If, on one of our strolls together through Hartswood, he had quietly advised me to put the brakes on my marriage plans for a while, I would have listened. I might have argued, but I'd have listened.

Why, in the last months of his life, did he fall into such melancholy introspection about his relationship with me? I had no hint of it at the time and it grieves me now to think he was afraid he might be losing his son's affection. Nothing could have been further from the truth. I loved and trusted him completely. Increasingly I relished the way I could speak to him on equal terms, as my boyhood slipped away behind me.

Now, I think the insecurity instilled in him during his childhood was whispering to him again. Since he was a boy he had been chronically sensitive to rejection. Denstone had put the tin lid on it. Perhaps he thought he was trapped in a closed loop, beginning and ending with renunciation. His father had pushed him away, now his son was about to do the same.

Of course I wasn't. Time would have proven this but there wasn't much of that left, not for him. So Dad kept his counsel and I blithely went my own way.

Meanwhile, the Madeleys were preoccupied. As Chris's last months swirled and washed away during a rainy spring, all our unknowing eyes were fixed upon the summer ahead. It was to be the occasion of not one, but two family nuptials: mine, and my sister's.

We didn't know that a third church service would close the season with a dark flourish.

Nineteen seventy-seven was shaping up to be quite a summer. Two weddings and a funeral.

*

My sister was married that June. Elizabeth's was a big, jolly, family affair – the Shawbury Madeleys came down to Brentwood en masse and Geoffrey played the organ for his granddaughter in the crowded church.

By contrast, there were just four guests in the little rural chapel where Lynda and I swore our vows to each other on the last Saturday in July – my parents, and the bride's mother and stepfather. The happy couple were insistent: no big ceremony, no best man, no bridesmaids. We decided to invite our parents only at the last minute.

Looking back, it's pretty obvious what was going on. We were unsure of ourselves; not at all certain this marriage was wise. Intuitively, we didn't want too many witnesses to the official start of what could turn out to be a serious mistake. It was almost like being in a new play that has had shaky rehearsals. You'd rather your friends and family stayed away on opening night.

But we crashed on regardless and emerged, slightly dazed, into the hot summer sunshine outside the church. A few snaps were taken and then it was across to the pretty little town of Cockermouth for the wedding breakfast. Table for six.

It was the last-but-one occasion I would see my father alive.

After lunch Lynda and I headed down to Shropshire and the ancient Feathers Hotel in Ludlow for our wedding night. My parents, who had driven up from Brentwood very early that morning, put up at our place on the edge of the fells. After breakfast my father drove 350 miles back home to Essex, dropped off my mother, filled up the tank and headed north again to Manchester. He had a gruelling week ahead making presentations all over the country for a big Ford PR push.

It was a chaotic schedule. I have his year planner for 1977 in front of me now, open at the first week in August. The diary shows him crazily criss-crossing Britain like a bluebottle in a room. Dad cursed the organisers who had arranged for him to drive from Manchester straight back down to London, on to Kent, back north to Harrogate, south again to Birmingham, and finally, on Friday the 5th, hundreds of miles north to Glasgow. He made his last speech there late in the afternoon and immediately called my mother.

'Right, that's it, I'm finished. I'm not staying away from you one more bloody night – I'm coming home. Should be back around midnight if the roads are OK.'

He sounded dog-tired to my mother. I was in the room as she spoke to him (Lynda and I were flat broke and were eking out our honeymoon with two or three days at my parents' house before going to Somerset). I could hear the concern in her voice as she said, 'Chris, you sound exhausted. You'll fall asleep at the wheel. Stay up there in Scotland tonight and get your sleep. You can come back in the morning.'

'No, I want to come home tonight. You know how much I've been missing you, Mary. It's been horrible without you this week. Anyway, Richard's heading off to Somerset tomorrow and I'd like to see him before he goes. Who knows when he'll be back again.'

'But Chris –'

'Stop worrying. I know my limits. Anyway, Friday's the best night of the week on Radio Four – I can listen to it most of the way down. That'll keep me alert. Stop worrying . . . I'll see you later.'

Next morning I came downstairs to find him sitting at the breakfast table.

'Hi, Dad – how are you feeling? You look knackered.'

'Well, that's how most of us look after an eight-hour drive at the end of a ghastly week. Anyway, how's marriage? When are you both pushing off to Somerset?'

And so our last conversation together slowly spooled out over tea and toast and the Saturday papers. I can't recall much of what we talked about, but I remember him teasing me about my car, an ancient left-hand-drive Citroën 2CV I'd just imported from Belgium.

'What are you doing driving a French tin can like that? I'm ashamed to have it in the drive . . . can't you park it round the corner when you come down? You should get yourself a Ford. Haven't you heard about honouring your father? Tsk, tsk.'

'At least my car wasn't designed in a dump like Detroit.'

And so on.

My last sight of my father is in reverse image. I'm looking at him in my rear-view mirror as I nose my battered, chugging car out of the drive and down the road between the spreading trees. He is standing on the pavement, one arm round my mother, the other waving a vigorous goodbye. Both her arms are wrapped around his waist. For once he is not wearing his Saturday suit but an old cricket jumper. Shirt and tie underneath, though.

I have rolled back the Citroën's striped canvas top and am waving my left hand high in the air in return. With the top down and windows open, I can just hear his final words to me, fading and falling with the Doppler effect as I pick up speed.

'Call that a car? You won't make the North Circular in that . . . I'll be towing you back here in an hour.'

And then we're rolling down the hill to Seven Arches Bridge and he's gone, slowly bobbing further and further behind me in the backwash of my life. Forever gone.

*

Lynda had become very fond of my father. Her own parents had divorced years before, and she was not especially close to the man her mother had gone on to marry. Her own father had retired to a far corner of northwest Scotland and she saw little of him. So she made a point of getting on with my dad. He always responded warmly to people who liked him and they had a friendly, easy relationship.

Unlike the one I had with my new wife on the first day of the second instalment of our honeymoon. We spent it on a beach looking out over Bridgewater Bay. We'd had an ugly row the night before – a trivial disagreement which spiralled into a worryingly intense conflict, a sign of things to come – and were still subdued when we arrived back at our holiday camp, which was tucked into a fold of the Mendip Hills.

A torn piece of notepaper had been pinned to the door of our little chalet. 'Mr Madeley – please phone home urgently.'

There were no mobile phones in 1977 so I had to walk into the nearby village to find a public call box. While I waited for the giggling girl inside to get off the phone, I ran through the possibilities. None of them were particularly encouraging. I couldn't think of one good reason why my parents would need to contact me. I was sure it was bad news.

I caught the girl's attention and made dialling gestures, mouthing 'very urgent' at her. She put her tongue out and turned her back.

I decided the likeliest thing was that my grandfather had taken a turn for the worse. He had been diagnosed with cancer a few months earlier and most of his lower intestine was subsequently removed. He had just turned eighty and the oncologist at Shrewsbury Hospital gave the family a bleak prognosis; Geoffrey Madeley, he said, would be unlikely to see another birthday.

But we had begun to wonder if the consultant was being overly pessimistic. Geoffrey had looked surprisingly hale at Elizabeth's wedding and played Mendelssohn's 'Wedding March' with his customary gusto, all the stops pulled out and not a chord fluffed.

Perhaps, I thought now, we had been watching his last hurrah.

The girl hung up, scowling at me as she left the box. I dialled my parents' number and my mother picked up at once. She must have been sitting by the phone.

'Hi, Mum, it's me. What's happened?'

Before she could speak there was banging on the door behind me. 'Hang on a sec.'

It was the girl again. 'I left my comb in there. Give it me.'

'For fuck's sake . . .' I pushed it through a broken pane and turned back to the phone. 'Go on.'

I heard my mother take a couple of shallow breaths. Then she spoke in a calm, quiet voice.

'Your father died at one o'clock this afternoon, he was in my arms, it was a massive heart attack.'

Her sentence, delivered with the economy of a newsroom ticker tape, was a knockout punch.

I came to a few minutes later. I was standing a few feet from the phone box, fumbling for a cigarette and dropping matches over the pavement. My fingers were numb, my ears were ringing and my legs were giving way. I managed to stumble to a low wall and half-sit, half-collapse on it.

I don't know how long I was there but I began to get odd looks from passers-by. One man stopped. 'You all right, then?'

I wanted to say I was fine, it was only that my father had just died, I'd be OK in a minute. But I could only stare at him. He wandered off uncertainly.

After a few minutes I got some feeling back in my legs and the electric hum in my head faded. I stood up and walked slowly back to our holiday home.

When I came through the door, Lynda stared at me. 'Good God, you look terrible. What on earth's happened?'

'Dad's dead.'

It sounded to my ears as if I had just told the worst, wickedest lie of my life.

*

My father's sudden death was a detonation of shocking force, instantly punching a wide hole through the fabric of his family. Like the survivors of a surprise air raid, we wandered around in shock, peering into the smoking crater and trying to make sense of our abruptly ruined landscape.

We believed that a great cosmic mistake had been made. I walked the woods alone the day afterwards, looking up at an iron-grey sky through the green canopy and saying through grinding teeth: 'You take it back, God. You just fucking take it back, all right? You've fucked up and now you have to fix it. You can do anything, can't you? So fix this, you bastard. Fix it now.'

My sister, who had taken delivery of her bound wedding photographs a couple of days earlier, was seized by the irrational belief that the whole thing was some kind of elaborate joke organised by our father. He hadn't died at all; at any moment there would be a knock at the front door. We'd open it to see him standing there, grinning sheepishly as we dragged him inside, weeping and laughing in our relief.

My mother was mostly silent, except at night when she sobbed quietly for hours in her bed. She was very far away from us. One night I went in and held her hand. After a while she sat up and said a strange thing.

'I feel so sorry for him . . . he has such a long way to go and he's so tired and frightened. Poor Chris . . .' Later, she would have no memory of saying this or what it might have meant.

My mother must have felt horribly alone. Both her parents had been dead for years. Her Canadian family was scattered across North America. Both her children were married, and one of them lived at the other end of the country. Now her husband had been torn from her side without so much as an hour or even a minute to prepare herself.

In an instant she had become a housewife without a husband. It was a catastrophe.

There was no word from Geoffrey or Kitty.

Up at Kiln Farm, a great silence had fallen.

*

The chief mourners were in fits of laughter. The widow was dabbing at her eyes with a tissue; the deceased's children were doubled up. Ahead of their black limousine, the hearse, with its flower-decked coffin, reversed awkwardly again from the cemetery entrance. The driver had almost hit the stone gateposts twice as he tried to drive between them; now he was lining up for his third attempt. He couldn't understand it. He had made this simple right-hand turn dozens, perhaps hundreds, of times. Why couldn't he manage it today?

We knew. Woodman Road Cemetery lay along the route of Chris and Mary Claire's nightly post-dinner walk; a mile or two of gentle exercise before bed.

My father had a superstitious dread of cemeteries. He hated going into them and was uncomfortable even walking past them. He always insisted on crossing the street to the pavement on the far side of Woodman Road Cemetery, much to his wife's amusement.

We used to tease him about his phobia. 'Go on, Dad, be a man. Walk there after sunset.'

'Laugh all you want,' he said, 'but I'm never going in there.'

We were laughing now as Thos. Bennett & Sons, Funeral

Directors and Undertakers, struggled to get their reluctant passenger through the gates. The driver finally made it at the fourth go, scraping a wing on the way.

When I explained things to him afterwards, he sighed with relief. 'Thank God for that,' he said. 'I couldn't understand it. It felt like a giant hand was pushing my hearse back. Mind you, sir, that's not the first time the dear departed have played their tricks on us, and it won't be the last I'm sure. I've seen and felt stranger things in cemeteries, I can tell you.'

I doubt he exaggerated. Many years later I brought Judy to see my father's grave. It was a long time since I'd been back and to my embarrassment I couldn't remember where he lay. There was no attendant to ask and after a while I thought we'd just have to go home again. Then Judy pointed. 'There he is. He's just over there.'

She was looking across to the far side of the cemetery. It was impossible to read what was on the gravestones from this distance, but I trudged over with her anyway. And there it was, the pale marble headstone engraved in gold letters: 'Christopher Holt Madeley, b. May 2 1928, d. August 8 1977'.

'How the bloody hell did you know it was here?'

My wife slowly shook her head. 'I have absolutely no idea. I just felt a sudden, complete certainty that this was the spot. How weird . . .'

As the man who drove my father's hearse said, strange things happen in graveyards.

*

Geoffrey didn't come to Chris's funeral. The silence that had fallen like a thick shroud over Kiln Farm persisted. Kitty, too, stayed away. There were no phone calls, no letters or cards, still less flowers. My Uncle Jim telephoned to explain. His parents, he said, were immobile with sorrow. The loss of a second son had almost paralysed them, coming as it did towards the closing years of their own lives, a cruel, cruel blow.

My grandparents were speechless and almost motionless with grief. They could barely make it downstairs in the morning, let alone down south to another funeral for a son, dead before his time.

I visited them at Shawbury, often, in the months and years that followed. They never spoke his name to me, unless by mistake, when they seemed to confuse me with him. This happened mostly with my grandmother, usually about an hour or so after I had arrived. They would listen politely to my news and answer my questions about them coherently, if briefly, and then Kitty would drift back down the years, usually settling in the 1940s and 50s.

'You love Denstone, don't you, darling? You were so glad Father and I sent you there . . .'

'Grandma, it's me, Richard, Chris's son.'

'Yes, of course . . . I'm sorry. That was a long time ago . . . Are you still with that paper in Tillsonburg? Why have you come home? Are you tired of Canada?'

And so on. Geoffrey rarely joined in these dreamlike conversations, but he never corrected his wife. I don't think he ever really thought I was his dead son but he seemed to take some comfort from the exchanges, especially when I went along with the delusion and answered as my father. I tried to remember his diplomatic evasions on the subject of Denstone and did my best to replicate them.

These peculiar discussions usually ended in the same way; Kitty would give a little sigh and suddenly say, 'But of course, you're not Chris at all . . . you're Richard. I'm so sorry, darling . . . are you staying here tonight or have you taken rooms at the Elephant?' The Elephant and Castle was an old inn with rooms in the middle of Shawbury. And we were all back in the present.

Meanwhile, Geoffrey's present was one of rude good health, generally speaking. He seemed indestructible. The bowel cancer that his gloomy doctors had predicted would carry him off a couple of years earlier had gone into full remission, never to return. One of his retinas had detached, giving him mono-vision to accompany his mono-hearing, but he still efficiently – and legally – drove a car. He listened to music on the stereo my father had bought him, and he played his baby grand. He continued to go on his walks across the fields.

Outwardly, my grandfather went on exactly as before Christopher's death. But I will never know what his inner responses to my father's sudden passing were, because he never talked about them. Did he berate himself for withholding his affections from the young, bespectacled schoolboy growing up in pre-war Shawbury? Did he question that iron-willed, immutable decision to banish his son to a grim boarding school in Staffordshire's sticks? Did he wish, with all his heart, that he'd at least once told his third-born that he loved him?

I don't know, partly because I didn't ask. I couldn't ask. I was still in my twenties and had barely begun to reflect on the paths the fathers and sons before me had been forced, or had chosen, to walk. Questions or comments about my father were always met with the same, urbane, closed-down response from my grandfather.

'Ah yes, Chris . . . let's talk about that another time, shall we?'

Meanwhile my grandmother gradually stopped confusing me with her dead son and merely looked puzzled when his name was mentioned.

My father, in death, hadn't exactly become Kiln Farm's equivalent of a Stalinist non-person. But like his baby brother John, death excommunicated him almost entirely from his parents' conversation. Banishment was the only way they could cope with two hammer blows that had struck at the beginning and the end of their marriage.

Geoffrey and Kitty would outlive my father by seven years. Kitty slowly sank into confusion. Towards the end she would telephone her son Jim in the middle of the night telling him breathlessly that there was a 'strange man' in the house. This was my grandfather, sleeping peacefully in his own bed next to hers.

Shortly before she had to be taken into care, I went to see her. We sat together in front of the tiled hearth above which Elizabeth and I had hung our Christmas stockings so many years before, and watched pictures in the fire.

I thought she had fallen asleep and was about to remove her glasses gently when suddenly her head jerked up and she stared at me intently.

'What is it, Grandma?'

Her eyes were full of tears but bright and fierce too.

'They're together, you know. John and Chris, I mean. They're playing right now in a meadow on the other side of the Wrekin.'

Perhaps they are.

*

Kitty died of heart failure. Geoffrey succumbed to a stroke. His deepest feelings about Henry's and William's betrayals went with him to the grave, as did his reflections on what sort of a father he had made. He died as he had lived, in near-inscrutable, dignified emotional privacy. I came to love him very much. I still miss him.

I have sometimes wondered what kind of a eulogy my father would have delivered had he been at his father's funeral. But that inner question is always subsumed by another. What would Chris have made of his own son; a man of twenty-eight with a new woman by his side; a woman who had just agreed to marry him?

And to trust him to be a step-parent to her children: seven-year-old twins. Twin boys.

What kind of a stepfather, my father might have wondered, would his son make?

On the day of Geoffrey's funeral, this was a question that had been occupying me for many months.

Chapter 10

———

FATHER AND SONS

'I come in a three-pack.'

Judy's reply when I asked her to marry me could not have been clearer. She was letting me know what I was in for.

The twins, Tom and Dan, were six, children of her first marriage to David. That marriage, like my own, had come to grief. But there was never a moment's argument or doubt who the boys would be living with. So if I wanted Judy, it would be a package deal – and I had to be absolutely certain I could handle that. So did she. I was still in my mid-twenties, after all; was I really up to the job of stepfather? We both had our doubts.

We'd realised we were falling for each other sometime in the spring of 1983. I had joined Granada Television in Manchester the previous year, as the third person in a line-up fronting the popular nightly regional news show *Granada Reports*. The other two presenters were Tony Wilson and Judy Finnigan.

Tony Wilson was a local legend – his lifestyle at that time was later the plotline for Steve Coogan's film *24 Hour Party People*. He was known as Mr Manchester. He was known as a lot of things – graffiti around town proclaimed that 'Tony Wilson is a wanker'. It delighted him and when I asked why he didn't mind, he said, 'Because it's true, I am a wanker. I'm a television presenter, aren't I? We're all wankers. Including you.'

Tony described presenting *Granada Reports* as 'my day job' and it was true. His other life was at the heart of the emerging 'Madchester' music scene. Tony launched bands like Happy Mondays and Joy Division, later renamed New Order, and ran the hippest club in the north, The Hacienda.

He was the most nerveless television presenter I ever knew, and stood completely outside the petty, potty world of television politics. Once, while he was reading the news, electricians doused the studio lights, part of some wildcat industrial action or other. Tony, forewarned, whipped out a penlight and carried on in the gloom without missing a beat. But timid management decided to pull the programme anyway and the cameras shut down. Tony went berserk, running into the director's gallery to confront startled producers.

'What the *fuck* are you doing? That was *great* television, you tossers!' When they told him the order to take him off-air had come from the great man himself, legendary Granada TV boss David Plowright, Tony marched straight to the lifts and punched the button for the executive floor.

He marched straight into Plowright's office without knocking.

The row that followed could be heard two floors down.

But Tony was probably the only television presenter not to be sacked for calling the managing director a c***.

Tony made his own chemistry. But the producers quickly decided that Judy and I were generating a subtler brand and Tony cheerfully went off to other shows while Granada built their news programme around the two of us.

They had no idea what kind of 'chemistry' they were promoting. Before long we both realised we had found in each other the person we wanted to spend the rest of our lives with. This was no office fling. Within a week of our first secret date I asked Judy to marry me. Her response was conditional. She told me she loved me but was dreading the impact of her pending divorce on her children, and had no intention of making matters worse by foisting an inept stepfather on them. She asked me to think it over very seriously and then tell her honestly if I thought I could hack it. If I had any doubts, the marriage was off. Pretending I was up for the role of stepfather would be pointless; it would quickly become evident that I wasn't fully committed and this second marriage for both of us would end disastrously.

I booked a fortnight's holiday and flew to Greece to sit on a beach and think it through. I only took hand luggage and my bag was heavy with books on step-parenting.

I should have saved myself the bother. As I sat on the sand under the fierce summer sun, I realised my books were useless, a horrible blend of 1980s psychobabble and nascent political correctness. Step-parents, I read, should not under any circumstances attempt to love their new partner's children. They should aspire to be no more than a friend; an extra listening ear in the family. Children would be confused by a deeper emotional commitment.

I thought this was utter guff then and I do now. Children have an infinite capacity to be loved – the more the merrier. My sad books made step-parenting sound like an exercise in timidity and frigid emotional withholding. Christ, this was exactly what Geoffrey and Chris had experienced during their childhoods and much good it had done them. I had no intention of inflicting such claptrap on Tom and Dan, if I was indeed to become their stepdad.

I walked back from the beach and tipped the books into the communal rubbish bin at the end of the dusty lane leading to my little taverna. Clearly, this was something I was going to have to work out for myself.

I have never forgotten that fortnight in Greece. I made a few friends but kept mostly to myself. I went on long walks to remote beaches whose sands bore the telltale marks showing that turtles had dragged themselves ashore in the night to lay their eggs. As I walked, I built endless models of the future in my head and demolished them with questions. Was I mature enough to be a stepfather? Was it something I actually wanted? Did I have the patience to handle the situation if the boys resented my arrival in their lives? Had I fully grasped what I was taking on?

I knew Tom and Dan slightly because Judy sometimes brought them to work with her. They were sweet-natured boys, blond and amenable. Being twins, they had a certain cachet. They called me Richard from the first day we met – they were used to seeing me on television with their mother – and sometimes they sat on my desk and told me dreadful jokes about superheroes. They were dedicated fans of the TV series

The A-Team and would earnestly enquire if I thought Mr T would prevail in a fight with Batman, should the two ever meet and happen to fall out.

'Mr T would win, I should think,' I extemporised.

'Why?'

'Well, er, he looks stronger than Batman to me. And he was a soldier in Vietnam so he knows how to fight.'

'What's Veetnim?'

'A place where there was a big war once.'

'Who won?'

'The army that Mr T's army was fighting.'

'That's silly, Mr T never loses fights. And he loves children.'

During these early encounters I found it impossible to tell the boys apart. Tom had a tiny freckle on the side of his nose but other than that they looked identical. It would be years before they would deliberately choose different hairstyles to mark themselves apart. But they never seemed to mind when I mixed them up. They were used to it, and anyway, as I say, both had easy-going natures.

Now, hundreds of miles away, I wondered if I could come to love these children. I certainly loved their mother.

I took a break from all the agonising and learned to windsurf. My tutor, a German, only had two words of English. 'Get vind! Get vind!' he bellowed from the surf as my sail flapped use-lessly at the wrong angle. And then when I did manage to catch the breeze, I'd promptly fall off. At least the sea was warm.

After two or three days of public ignominy, I suddenly found I was able to tack back and forth across the little bay and even manage to steer around swimmers in my way. I thanked my teacher and paid him his final drachmas. He nodded and smiled something in German. I asked his girlfriend, who spoke English, what he'd said.

'He says his work here is done,' she laughed. 'He doesn't mean the windsurfing. He means that he's made you happy. We've been watching you, you know. You always looked so sad.'

'No, no,' I said. 'I've just got a rather important decision to make, that's all. I'm not sad, honestly. Just a bit thoughtful.'

That night I took my blankets down on to the deserted beach. There was no moon and the sky glowed with stars and planets and distant, fuzzy galaxies. As I stared into infinity my mind, unbidden, made a soft, unmistakable click. Like a computer fed a stream of complex information ending with a question mark, my subconscious had, in its own time, delivered its answer.

Of course I could be a stepfather to the twins. Of course. I already liked them and suddenly felt a surging confidence that I could love them, too. The practicalities would work themselves out; the most important thing was to put the happiness of the boys first. Judy already did that; if I followed suit, everything would fall into place.

Like the answer to most problems, the solution was devastatingly simple once you grasped it.

I walked back to my room. The power was off, so I had to write my letter to Judy by candlelight.

Then I went to bed and slept until noon.

*

'How much longer are you going to be?'

Judy's voice came out of the dusk of an early August evening. I dropped the spanner I was holding on to the drive and wearily adjusted the angle of the big square torch on the roof of my two-door, two-litre Ford, currently undergoing its metamorphosis from single man's car-about-town into family saloon.

'Fuck knows. Nothing seems to fit, and I think there are some screws missing. I'll probably have to use wire or something . . . maybe half an hour if I can get these runners to stay put.'

I was transforming too, from fastback driver into roof-rack dad. Holidays for one – or two at most – were over. Tomorrow would see the start of a holiday for me and the three-pack. The famous four – Richard, Judy, Tom and Dan – were about to go wild in Cornwall.

My sports saloon only had room for a couple of toothbrushes and a bottle of Calpol in its ridiculous boot. Hence the roof rack, hastily bought an hour earlier and now stubbornly resisting all attempts to assemble it in the gathering gloom of a Manchester evening.

'You should have done it earlier. Would you like a gin and tonic out here, or shall I leave it in the kitchen? I'm going to bed. We've got an early start . . .'

We'd made our plans a few weeks earlier. My final divorce papers had come through and Lynda and I were free to go our separate ways. It had been a rocky marriage with too many rows, and we'd finally split a year and a half earlier, soon after Christmas 1982. There had never been any real question of having children: we didn't get on well enough. The whole thing was a damn shame. But Lynda married again – a farmer in North Yorkshire – and bore him a baby girl.

Meanwhile Judy and David were now separated. In return for the deeds to their home, a pretty detached house opposite Manchester Grammar School in Old Hall Lane, David was freed of any future financial responsibilities for the boys. I had promised to share these, and the mortgage, with Judy. A lot of trust was involved on all sides and later I had to repeat my pledges to a judge in the family courts.

Meanwhile there was the pressing question of how to introduce myself to Tom and Dan, now seven, as a permanent fixture in their lives. Judy and I decided that after a series of days out together – at the end of which I modestly returned to my nearby flat – we should advance matters by renting a holiday cottage in Cornwall, where the boys could get used to me being around at bedtime and for breakfast. If all went well, I would move in to Old Hall Lane when we got back.

I finally got the roof rack bolted on at about one in the morning and crept into the spare room with my flat G&T. This was it, then. Moment of truth, and all that. Tomorrow – no, today – I would assume a hands-on paternal role for the first time. David, of course, was the boys' father – and a constant and crucial force in their lives to this day – but I was on the final descent to touchdown on what a friend in similar circumstances called 'Planet Steppy'.

I knew from those dumped reference books that there were

no reliable guides or maps; I would have to find my own way, and I fought back a sudden frisson of panic.

This was no time to go flaky on a mother and her two boys.

*

We broke the journey from Manchester to Cornwall at a small family hotel in Somerset, close to the village where I'd received the news of my father's death. I wondered what he would have made of his son's great big adventure; a holiday to the West Country and the start of a whole new chapter in my life. I think he would have been intrigued. He certainly would have been relieved to see that I was at last driving a Ford.

'We mustn't sleep in the same room tonight,' Judy told me firmly as we checked in. 'I think it'd be a really good idea if you share with the boys. They'll think it's fun, all guys together. I'll take a single.'

Most of the conversation at dinner that evening was taken up with comparing the relative merits of superheroes. Judy and David must have heard it all a hundred times before but at least I was fresh to the debate and engaged with mostly unfeigned enthusiasm. Judy stifled a yawn.

'OK, boys, that's it. Cornwall tomorrow, bed now. You know where your room is – I'll be up to tuck you in a minute. So will Richard.'

I looked at her as they disappeared up the stairs. 'So . . . how d'you think it's going so far?'

'If I'd realised you knew so much about Batman, Spiderman and the Green Goblin I'd never have agreed to marry you.

Seriously, darling, it's going better than I could have hoped. Don't feel you have to try too hard with them, though. When you're fed up talking about bloody superheroes, just tell them.'

'Er . . . right, I will.'

I didn't tell her I'd kept my best stuff about Spiderman back for the next round.

*

I look back now on those ten days in Cornwall with a kind of reverence. They were among the most perfect days of my life. The August sunshine was absurdly extravagant; we lived under a bowl of brilliant blue from dawn to dusk. At night we and the boys would lie out on the little lawn in front of our cottage and watch satellites coursing silently between the stars. Meteorites flared brightly as they rushed to their doom, and once, a tumbling green shooting star eerily lit our upturned faces.

During the days, cornfields that crowded to the sea cliffs shone bright yellow in the sun, and great clouds of dust rose like smoke as the giant combines brought in the harvest. Despite the warm nights we lit log fires and candles and read the boys Cornish ghost stories and legends.

One sultry afternoon Judy took a siesta and I took her sons to Lantic Bay, one of the most stunning cliff-beaches in Britain. There is no access by car and we hiked the mile or so to the steep, rocky path that plunges down from the dizzy cliffs that half-circle the sandy cove. When we got to the bottom it was low tide and we plucked baby mussels from the exposed rocks, planning to simmer them with onions and wine and cream in a home-made moules marinière. Dan, at seven, was already something of a gastronome. He'd try anything on a restaurant menu and never forgot what it was called.

Then I had second thoughts – specifically, thoughts about shellfish poisoning – and we dropped the little creatures back in their rock pool. Years later I harvested Lantic's mussels again, and this time defiantly took them home and cooked them. They were delicious.

It was the first time I had spent more than a few minutes alone with the twins. Until now, our relationship had been conditioned, to a certain extent, by their mother's presence. This didn't occur to me until we were clambering back up the cliffs to get to our car, and I reviewed the past few hours. We'd had a good time . . . hadn't we?

'Had a good time, boys?' I shouted after them as they raced each other to the stile at the top of the path.

'Yes!' they yelled over their shoulders.

Mind you, I thought, you can't go wrong if you put a boy on a beach.

That night we had a barbecue and after the boys had gone to bed, stuffed with my best burned sausages, Judy and I took our drinks out into the cottage's little garden.

'How did it go today with the boys?'

I shrugged. 'Unselfconsciously, I guess. We had fun.'

'Did they talk about their dad?'

'Yes, a bit. Not to make a point or anything, I don't think – they were just telling me about stuff they do with him. It was fine, honestly.'

The rental on our cottage ran out, but none of us wanted to

go home so we squeezed an extra couple of days out of our holiday and checked into a hotel at nearby Talland Bay. They only had their two most expensive rooms left, but we took them anyway, mouthing not entirely unfeigned horror at each other about the cost when the receptionist's back was turned. Next day, in the hotel pool, Tom and Dan shouted across to two new friends they had made.

'How much did your room cost? Ours cost a hundred pounds!'

Mortifying.

Our almost dreamlike interlude over, we rolled back into Manchester on a Sunday evening and I carried everyone's bags back into the house in Old Hall Lane.

'Right . . . well . . . that's everything, I think . . . I'll just, er . . .'

The twins looked up at me in surprise.

'Aren't you staying?'

I looked at their mother. 'What do you think?'

Judy smiled. 'I think that would be fine.'

*

One morning at breakfast, after a couple of weeks at Old Hall Lane, Dan asked through a mouthful of Ready Brek: 'Is it all right that Tom and me call you Richard?'

'Yes, of course. You can call me whatever you want. Why?'

'Cos some of our friends at St James's' – a primary school at the end of the road where the boys went – 'have stepdads too and they call them Daddy, but that's what we call our Daddy.'

'I know. Maybe your friends' real fathers don't see them any more, not like your daddy does. I think you should just carry on calling me Richard.'

'I know,' said Tom. 'We can call you Steppy.'

The boys thought this was highly amusing, so Steppy I was for a month or two before the joke waned, and then we went back to Richard.

We were a daily presence in each other's lives now, so it was a huge stroke of fortune that we just happened to get along right from the start. I thought the boys were funny, good company, and interesting. Our holiday in Cornwall had been an inspired idea (Judy's) and a useful dress rehearsal for this new play in which we were all cast, a production that now seemed set to run daily until further notice.

There was almost a first-night disaster. We'd unpacked and Judy sent the boys to run their evening bath, a job they insisted on doing for themselves. After a couple of minutes there was a yelp from upstairs and Dan ran to the banisters.

'Richard, there's a massive spider in the bath. Come and get it, please.'

I grabbed a thick magazine and went upstairs to do my duty.

But there was to be no execution that night. The boys were horrified when I prepared to crush the impressively large creature crouching near the plughole.

'No! You mustn't kill it! Daddy never kills them! You have to pick it up and throw it out of the window.'

I loathed spiders. Not quite phobic about them, I nevertheless couldn't go to sleep in a bedroom with one on the wall. It had to be despatched before lights out.

The prospect of reaching down and picking this monster up

with my bare hands was stomach-churning. But it was clearly a test sent by God. 'So you want to be a stepfather, do you, matey? Let's see how you handle this, then . . . their real father could . . .'

Fuck, I had no choice. 'Right, well, if that's what Daddy does, I'd better do the same.' I opened the window, and considered the spider. It considered me. It looked rather smug now, I thought, still hesitating.

'Go on! We want our bath!'

Bugger it. I reached down, grabbed the creature by the legs and hurled it out of the window in one sweeping motion.

'There. All done.' I swaggered out of the bathroom.

Downstairs, I boasted to Judy. 'You know I hate spiders? Well I just picked up an *enormous* one with my bare hands. I didn't think I had it in me. I think I might have actually cured my fear of them. I –'

'Oh, for God's sake. David did it all the time and never made a fuss. Honestly . . .'

Trickier to handle than spiders in the bath was the potentially fraught area of discipline. I dreaded hearing the words: 'You can't tell us what to do, you're not our dad,' and in those early weeks and months I trod very carefully, leaving most laying down of the law to their mother, although this was pretty much the normal state of affairs anyway. The boys were used to fairly long periods without their father at home – he was a successful documentary programme maker and was often abroad filming – and Judy was very much the one in charge.

In any case, I had to accept that I was new at the parenting game and had a lot to learn. I took my cues from her.

One of the first things I noticed was how adroit she was at avoiding confrontation. Tom was going through a phase of developing mild addictions to foods and his current obsession was with the fruit drink Five Alive. He could get through cartons of the stuff in one sitting, if allowed. I suggested not buying any more for a while, but Judy disagreed.

'He'd just move on to something else. It's only a phase; he has to learn self-control, that's all.'

But the lure of Five Alive was too much for seven-year-old Tom. Like the Secret Lemonade Drinker in the TV ads, he was drawn to the fridge like a moth to the flame. One night, soon after the boys had been put to bed, stealthy noises could be heard coming from the kitchen. Judy went in and there was the criminal, dressed in Superman pyjamas, guzzling his fix straight from the carton.

'Tom!'

He leaped in the air like a startled cat and raced up the stairs to bed. Judy called after him: 'And no more tonight, Tom, that's an order. And stay in bed.'

A few minutes later there was a creak from the stairs. We crept to the door and peered out. It was Superman again, tiptoeing with pantomime steps across the hall to the kitchen. Judy swept out like an inshore patrol boat intercepting contraband.

This time the raiding party was escorted to the room he shared with his brother and given a firm telling-off. But a few minutes after Judy had come down again, there was a knock on the living-room door. It was Dan.

'Tom won't let me go to sleep. He keeps crying and shouting, "I want Five Alive." It's giving me a headache.'

We went upstairs. The noises coming from the boys' bedroom made it sound as if Tom had been left lashed to the rack; sobs and bellows interspersed with the mangled mantra: 'Wa – nt – Fi – ve – Al-Al-Alive!'

I turned to Judy, trying to keep a straight face. 'It's a battle of wills. This is your Cuban missile crisis; you can't blink first. Ask yourself: what would Kennedy have done?'

'Shut up, I'm trying to think . . .'

Hearing our voices, Tom ratcheted up the volume. '*F-F-Five Alive!*'

'You can't give in to him, Judy.'

She brightened. 'No – but I can negotiate, like your precious Kennedy. Go get the bloody Five Alive and an eggcup.'

By the time I was back Tom had stopped wailing and was sitting up in bed, hiccupping and sniffling. Judy sat next to him, holding his hand. She turned to me with her serious face on. 'I've explained to Tom why he can't keep drinking Five Alive all the time and he's promised to only have two glasses a day from now on. To show we trust him, I've said he can have an eggcup of it before he goes to sleep tonight. Pour it out, would you?'

So the brimming thimble was solemnly handed over and Tom took five minutes to slowly sip it dry.

Downstairs again, I asked Judy if she thought the Five Alive pledge would hold.

She seemed surprised at my question. 'Of course. The boys always keep their promises. You'll learn that for yourself.'

*

When did I realise that I had come to love the boys? As far as I can remember, I think it was three or four months after I stopped killing spiders. We'd all driven down from Manchester to my mother's house in rural Essex. She'd remarried a couple of years earlier and now lived with her new husband in his beautiful Tudor farmhouse just outside Danbury. It looked like something out of the property pages of *Country Life*.

My mother had met Jim in 1981, four years after my father died. She had been very lonely. So was Jim – his wife had died a few years previously, coincidentally of heart trouble. My mother had called to give me the news of her engagement as I was dashing out with a film crew to cover a breaking news story. I took the call in the studio reception.

'You'll have to be quick, Mum, I'm on a story. What is it?'

'Have I mentioned Jim at all?'

'Uncle Jim? What about him?'

She laughed. 'No, another Jim . . . we've been seeing each other a bit . . . well, quite a lot.'

I could guess what was coming.

'Anyway, last night he asked me to marry him and I said . . . well, I said yes. Do you mind?'

Did I mind? I was hugely relieved. I was still working up north, for Yorkshire Television at that time, and felt incredibly guilty that I didn't get back to see my mother more often. My blessings on her impending nuptials were extravagant.

Sadly the marriage was not to last. Jim died suddenly of a stroke in 1987. My mother would be a widow a second time.

But not for the last. A few years later, she met and married her third husband, Eric. Eric was an ex-commander in the

Metropolitan Police. He made my mother very happy, which was a blessing because her marriage to Jim had, in the end, turned sour. I never really knew exactly what went wrong between them, but shortly before Jim's stroke my mother was actively considering divorce.

Things must have been pretty bad. When I arrived at her house for Jim's funeral, she came out in the drive to meet me. She was in her widow's weeds and sundry mourners peered glumly from the windows of the house.

I walked across the gravel to greet her, stretching out my arms in sympathy. 'I'm so sorry, Mum . . .'

She embraced me and at the same time whispered in my ear, 'Meet the merry widow!'

Blimey. That bad.

Eric restored her faith in marriage. But they would have barely a decade together before cancer took him from her.

*

It was the first time Judy or my new stepsons had met my mother. I think, to be honest, I'd been putting it off until everything at Old Hall Lane had settled down. Everyone, including me, was slightly nervous as the car crunched up the gravel driveway and I pipped the horn to let our hosts know we'd arrived. I turned to look at the anxious little faces in the back.

'Don't worry. She's really nice. You'll like her – and Jim.'

'Is Jim your steppy?'

'Well, yes, but as I was explaining on the way here, it's a bit different from how it is with me and you. I was all grown-up when Jim met my mum and they decided to get married. I've never lived with him, like I do with you. He's a sort of . . . well, friend. I don't love him like I do you two.'

There. It was said.

And the twins merely took it as their due, nodding their understanding as they climbed out of the car. Casually telling them I loved them had made no more impact than if I'd said the sun was shining or today was Tuesday. That was because, I realised as I grabbed our cases and followed Judy and her sons into the old half-timbered house, my feelings for them had gradually become a fact of life as indisputable as the weather or the date.

Later, at dinner, Tom and Dan were on their unasked-for best behaviour. They were studiously polite, avoided the usual opportunities to bicker between themselves, and did their best to join in the conversation. When they offered to help clear away the plates and had disappeared for a few moments into the kitchen with my mother and her husband, I turned to Judy.

'Aren't the boys being amazing? Dinner was like a Norman Rockwell painting come to life . . . I've never known them be so good. I'm so proud of them.'

'That's because they want you to be. They may be little but they know this is a big deal for you. I'm incredibly proud of them too.'

Our first Christmas together came and went. The boys divided their time between us and their father, who was destined himself to remarry and have more children. Judy hated being apart from her sons, even for a few hours on Boxing Day, but the new arrangement seemed to be working. We both kept our radar alert for any signs of disturbance or unhappiness in the twins, but as the months passed they seemed as happy and tranquil as ever. The kind of rifts and crises in step-family set-ups that I'd read about and were, according to those glum self-help books, inevitable, refused to materialise. The boys seemed quite stable and there were no reports from their school of any behavioural problems.

Perhaps it helped that we'd decided not to move from Old Hall Lane for at least a year, much as we both wanted to. I always felt slightly awkward living in Judy's former marital home; I could hardly wait for us to make a completely fresh start somewhere else. But the boys' happiness was paramount and an early move might have destabilised them, so we stayed put for the time being.

The twins and I had our moments, certainly: the time Dan did something beyond the pale and I chased him from the kitchen into the front room. He grabbed a wooden chair and thrust it towards me like a lion-tamer, shouting, 'Back! Back!' We stared at each other for a moment before bursting out laughing.

But I can't remember any major crises or set-piece confrontations. The boys were usually biddable and co-operative, and always open to negotiation.

Who knows? Maybe we were doing things right. Maybe we were just lucky. As a stepfather, I was certainly exceptionally lucky in my stepsons. In terms of their characters and behaviour, they were a doddle.

Meanwhile I was getting a hell of a kick out of all the everyday, routine things – reading them their bedtime stories, driving them to school playing their favourite music cassette (which for months on end was the theme from the movie *Ghostbusters*. Every bloody morning. Whenever I hear it now I experience a vague anxiety about whether I've remembered to put both lunchboxes in the car).

I realised I had been incredibly fortunate. I'd drawn a Queen with Judy and two straight Jacks with her boys. What a hand. But there were new cards in the deck waiting to be dealt. In August 1985, exactly a year after that first family holiday in Cornwall, Judy said she had something to tell me.

She was pregnant.

Our first child was on the way. A son.

*

It wasn't the first time Judy had told me she was expecting our baby. In the early spring, she'd lost a pregnancy within a few days of showing positive on a home testing kit. But soon she was pregnant again and this time everything seemed to unfold normally. Two months became three and we were certain we could now see and feel her emerging bump.

At sixteen weeks she went in to St Mary's maternity hospital in Manchester for her first scan. The picture resolution wasn't as good back in the mid-80s as it is now, with today's extraordinarily sharp 3-D images, but we'd been given a few sample shots of other women's early scans and figured we knew what to look for in the fuzzy black-and-white ultrasound pictures.

The radiographer breezily introduced herself as Kath and

took Judy through to the examination room. 'I'll come and get you when it's all set up,' she called over her shoulder to me. 'Back in a few minutes.'

I leafed through some magazines and waited, incredibly excited. Ultrasound scans were pretty new back then – I'd never even heard of them, to be honest – and the thought that in a few moments we'd be looking at grainy images of our unborn child nestling in the womb was extraordinary.

Ten minutes became fifteen and still Kath hadn't returned. Perhaps, I thought, there was a problem with the machine. Perhaps –

'Mr Madeley . . . Richard . . . will you come through, please.'

The radiographer's voice had changed; she sounded quieter, serious. My heart began to beat a little faster, but not with excitement.

It was only a few steps to the curtained-off cubicle, and as we got there Kath turned and met my eyes.

'Look, it's not good,' she said quickly. 'It's not good at all.'

I swallowed. 'Has she lost the baby?'

'Not exactly . . . it's still there, obviously, but I'm very sorry to tell you that it seems to have died in the womb. I've sent for the consultant but I don't think there's anything we can do.'

I stared at her a moment and then pushed through the green curtains to find my wife in silent tears on the examination couch. She turned to me, eyes glistening. 'Richard, it's died . . . I'm sorry . . .'

The coming hours and days were extremely difficult for her. Once the radiographer's verdict had been confirmed, there was the deeply distressing business of trying to deliver a dead baby.

At first they tried to induce labour with drugs, but after a day or so it became clear that wasn't going to work. Judy's body was refusing to give up its tiny foetus.

They switched tactics and she was wheeled into theatre for an abortion; the termination of a pregnancy that had already privately concluded itself.

Afterwards, the consultant advised me to take my wife away for a few days, so Judy's mother Anne looked after the boys while we flew down to the Côte d'Azure.

It was as good a place as any to come to terms with what had just happened. But everywhere we looked there were babies. On the beach, in cafés, at our hotel; everywhere, all around us, all the time, babies, babies, babies.

*

St Mary's could find nothing seemingly wrong with our still-born child. He was a boy and appeared physically perfect. They estimated he'd died at around fifteen weeks from cause or causes unknown.

We were advised to keep trying. Kath confided in Judy that she too had lost a pregnancy in identical circumstances, and gone on to have healthy children. We quickly realised after conversations with friends and from a little basic research that early miscarriage and foetal death is incredibly common. In any case, at least it was clear Judy had no difficulty becoming pregnant, and she'd already carried twins to term.

We put our sadness behind us and tried to stop worrying.

Sure enough, three months later, Judy was expecting again.

The date for the first scan arrived. There was no excitement now as we drove to St Mary's, just a creeping dread we kept trying to push to the back of our minds. It was hard not to be fearful; there'd been no sign that anything was wrong the last time we arrived here.

It was Kath who greeted us again and this time she allowed me to come straight through to the scanning unit. As she spread the lubricating jelly on Judy's stomach and reached for the ultrasound camera, she smiled at us both. 'Don't worry. I'm sure it's all going to be fine.'

The grainy picture glowed into life on the screen above our heads and we held our breaths.

Kath sighed. 'Yes, there we are . . . see it?'

We craned our necks. Judy was first to comprehend. 'Is that it there? That little bean thing?'

Kath laughed. 'That's it.'

The child of the future seemed to be lazily bouncing up and down the screen, for all the world like one of those early Pacman computer-game figures.

'Is that normal?'

'As the day is long . . . Judy, you are very, very pregnant. Congratulations.'

When we got home, we showed the Polaroid Kath had given us to Tom and Dan.

'Wow. That's amazing,' they said, shaking their heads in wonder.

Later, their mother upstairs, we looked at the picture again.

'Can you really see the baby, boys?'

'No.'

'Me neither. But I promise it's there. You've got a brother or a sister on the way.'

It would be wrong to say the twins were excited about the prospect of a new baby in our home. They seemed genuinely pleased and curious, but not excited. Relaxed would be a better word. We'd been watching them carefully for any signs of incipient jealousy or resentment, but so far their day-to-day tranquillity seemed undisturbed.

One evening I came in from the garden after a game of football with them and flopped down in front of the television with Judy.

'What were you all laughing about out there?'

'Names. Names for the baby. Tom wants to call it Hannibal if it's a boy (*The A-Team* again); Dan prefers Face (more *A-Team*).'

'What if it's a girl?'

'That depends on how you spell "Yeuch".'

She laughed. 'They're very unfazed by all this, aren't they? What do you think? Honestly?'

I decided to go for it. 'I think it's time we stopped worrying about them so much on this. They're totally cool with it, Judy. You're a brilliant mother and they've grown up incredibly secure in themselves. They know how much we love them and it's blindingly obvious to me that they're not threatened by this baby. They're looking forward to it. I really think we should relax.'

But as her pregnancy developed, Judy suffered an endless series of crises of confidence. Not about her boys, not now, but about the baby inside her. Once it started kicking her anxiety lessened, only to swell up again during the inevitable periods when it lay still. Then she would be convinced that this child, too, had died. She had lost all confidence in her body's ability to nurture and nourish a growing foetus.

I did my best to comfort and reassure her but underneath a confident exterior I was as jumpy and superstitious as she. Sometimes, in the end, the only thing to do was drive across to St Mary's for another scan. Kath, who had become a friend, had left standing instructions that these were not to be denied, within reason. The results were always the same.

'His heartbeat is strong. He's just asleep in there. You've nothing to worry about, Judy.' Then a glance across at me. 'Or you.'

We knew by now we were having a boy, much to the twins' unabashed relief. A routine amniocentesis check (where fluid around the baby is drawn off for tests) had confirmed its sex, as well as its health. And as the pregnancy passed the seven-month point and a viable birth became possible, everyone relaxed, even Judy. It was going to be OK.

Suddenly, it was a time of birthdays. Tom and Dan turned nine in March. A few weeks afterwards I said goodbye to my twenties and three days later, on a Friday in May, Judy was thirty-seven. Now there was just the weekend to go before the next ring on the calendar was crossed off.

Monday, May the 19th.

I had done my best – was doing my best – as a stepfather.

What kind of a father would I make?

Chapter 11

———

GENERATION IV

Jack came out of Judy's belly like a free-falling parachutist, legs and arms braced wide, back arched. The umbilical added to the illusion, looking like a ripcord waiting to be pulled to release his canopy.

The operation to deliver him into the world was surprisingly violent, far more so than I had expected. Tom and Dan had been delivered by Caesarean too – there were potential complications to a natural birth – and so was their brother, as a large but benign cyst on one of his mother's ovaries required simultaneous removal. It was this cyst, we speculated, that had interrupted the blood supply to the placenta in Judy's previous pregnancy and caused it to fail. But who knows?

Judy wanted me to be present for the birth and as I am not at all squeamish about blood and operations I was more than happy to be there. I had pictured delicate incisions being made, careful openings into the womb fashioned, a gentle easing-out of the infant within . . .

It was more like a cross between a mugging and a smash-and-grab raid. Slash, clamp, slash, clamp, and then both the surgeon's hands were vigorously wrestling the baby into the open air. The operating table creaked and swayed under the onslaught. Judy, comfortably numb from her epidural anaes-thetic, stared at the starfish baby that suddenly dangled in the air above her.

'My God! There he is!'

All was bustle as our son was swept into the next room to be checked and de-gunged, while his mother's cyst was removed without ceremony. Faint squawks and mews heralded Jack's re-entry into the delivery room and suddenly I was holding a tightly blanketed baby in my arms, while his living quarters for the last nine months were swiftly clipped off and sewn shut.

The actor Peter Ustinov once said that his newborn daugh-ter's face had 'something of the secrecy and doggedness of a Soviet Field Marshal about it'.

As I lowered our swaddled son on to his mother's shoulder, I could see what Ustinov meant, although I thought there was more of Churchill in my son's expression than Zhukov. But there was something else; something more primitive in Jack's face as he snuffled and wheezed after nine comfortable months having had the trying business of oxygenating his own blood managed for him.

'He's beautiful, Judy.'

'Yes . . . he's perfect. Our son. What does he remind me of, though? I can't quite think.'

We considered him together. Suddenly Judy snorted with laughter.

'A dinosaur. That's it. His little face looks like a baby T-Rex before its teeth come in.'

It did, too. Jack, like his brothers, was destined to grow into a handsome lad but there was a distinctly prehistoric look about him in his earliest days, as if some crazed scientist had laced human DNA with a soupçon of reptile cells.

'It does not,' I lied. 'Maybe a little beaky, that's all . . . come on, he's only been in the fresh air five minutes. Give a velociraptor a break.'

And we laughed, suffused with happiness and relief. A draining nine months was over.

Judy's mother, Anne, was looking after Tom and Dan at home. Later, heading back to show them the Polaroid snaps of their mother and new brother, I found myself making a U-turn and driving back to the hospital. When I walked quietly into the ward again, the lights were low. Judy was fast asleep and so was our baby, wrapped in white blankets in the clear Perspex cot in the little nursery next door. Like my father before me, I stared and stared at my new-minted boy, scarcely able to believe in his existence. Finally a nurse ushered me out and fifteen minutes later I was showing my photographs to the excited twins in the kitchen at Old Hall Lane.

'What d'you think, then?'

Dan looked thoughtful.

'Honestly?'

'Honestly.'

'OK. How come he looks so old?'

'Because he's been floating in water for nearly a year. It's like your fingers and toes if you sit in the bath too long – they go all wrinkly. Everything will smooth out in a day or two.'

Tom picked up one of the pictures and studied it.

'Will he still look like a dinosaur?'

A couple of days later mother and baby were home. Suddenly, the unease I felt about living in Judy's former marital home intensified. I couldn't bear to live in this house much longer; it was redolent of a past that wasn't mine, and not an altogether happy one either.

Judy agreed and we put it on the market. We found a buyer straight away and took out an eye-watering mortgage on a big three-storey Edwardian house in nearby Didsbury. The twins seemed totally unfazed by the move, which for them included a transfer to a new school. Perhaps we could have upped sticks earlier, after all.

Our new home, on Old Broadway, had been built with families in mind. The whole street had. It was a graceful turn-of-the-century cul-de-sac, designed by a Russian émigré who had been inspired, apparently, by the elegant houses in St John's Wood in north London. In fact, whenever Granada Television wanted to re-create a leafy London look for one of its dramas, they filmed in our road.

A broad band of grass studded with mature trees ran down the centre of the street, which ended in a park. That meant there was no through traffic, so Old Broadway was popular with young families. In some ways the place felt like a throwback to another time; children of all ages played happily together in the street, unsupervised by grown-ups. 'This is what things were like before the war,' Judy's mother commented with approval.

The kids called themselves the Broadway Bombers; had done as far back as anyone could remember. They climbed the trees, built camps under the huge holly bushes that grew in a circle opposite our house, organised bicycle races and wandered in and out of each other's houses. In summer the place felt like a middle-class commune.

Perhaps the danger that finally penetrated our easy-going street was overdue; inevitable. One bright summer morning piercing screams rang through the air; terrible, blood-curdling cries.

They came from near one of the houses closest to the park. It was our friend and colleague Tony Wilson's home. He was away filming and in his absence catastrophe had arrived unannounced.

Tony didn't know it, but he had a stalker; a large, powerfully built woman who had become fixated on him. She had tracked the presenter to his house the night before, somehow got into the garage, and slept there. Tony had been picked up in the morning by a studio car, so his own was still in the garage. The woman thought the object of her obsession was still at home.

When she knocked on the door, it was opened by Tony's unsuspecting wife, Hilary. The woman told some tale about being an old friend of her husband; could she see him? They had so much catching up to do . . .

Hilary was completely taken in, and said with genuine regret, 'Oh, I'm really sorry, but he's not here – he's gone to work. He won't be back for hours, I'm afraid.'

'Oh, how disappointing . . . and I've come such a long way to see him again.'

Hilary, a generous soul, felt sorry for the woman on her doorstep and invited her inside for a coffee. She led the way into the kitchen and turned around to ask if she took milk and sugar.

Her visitor was now holding a Stanley knife. Without the slightest hesitation she stepped forward and slashed Hilary's face with it, and again, and again. Hilary's hands and arms were sliced open as she desperately tried to protect herself; eventually, half-blinded by her own blood, she managed to get away and run out through her front porch, screaming incoherently for help, her face in ribbons. Her attacker slammed the heavy door shut behind her.

Appalled neighbours ran towards Tony's stricken wife, and her screams suddenly became even louder.

'My baby's in there! Oh God, my baby's in there!'

Her son, only a few weeks old, was sleeping upstairs in the nursery.

So far, incredibly, the baby hadn't been woken by the uproar. The maniac downstairs was unaware that an infant slept, oblivious, directly above her. For the moment, at least.

Hilary, now almost unconscious from loss of blood and shock, was given emergency first aid on the pavement; shirts, jackets, anything that could be folded and pressed on to her wounds was applied before the ambulance arrived and rushed her to hospital. Meanwhile, police cars had roared up at the house and officers began negotiating with the intruder through the letter box. They made no mention of the baby and prayed they could talk the woman out before he woke up.

Her obsession with Tony Wilson quickly became apparent

and the officers immediately used it as a psychological lever to get her to open the door.

'Come out of the house and you can talk to Tony,' they promised. 'He's on his way, but you have to come out if you want to see him. He won't want to talk to you through his own letter box, will he, love?'

The ruse worked. Eventually the door slowly opened and there she stood, docile, drenched in Hilary's blood.

From upstairs came the faint but unmistakable cries of a baby waking up. It had been that close.

Hilary survived and, amazingly, recovered her pretty looks. She made valiant attempts to overcome the trauma, although understandably this took time. Her attacker was sectioned indefinitely. The atmosphere in the road changed abruptly.

Old Broadway's easy-going open-door culture evaporated overnight. Security chains, which had long dangled, unused, were oiled and clicked into place; vans belonging to burglar alarm companies were seen parked in the street. The Broadway Bombers were grounded until further notice. Tony's on-screen colleagues – ourselves included – found themselves looking uneasily over their shoulders, as many presenters did thirteen years later after Jill Dando's brutal murder.

But things almost always return to normal faster than most of us think they will. After a few months of uneventful tranquillity, Old Broadway began to breathe easily again. The Bombers were allowed back on the street and up in the trees.

And Hilary had another baby. A girl.

*

That autumn we took the boys and the baby to the Canaries for a fortnight. Judy, the twins and me came back with suntans.

Jack returned with black eyes and bruises. I had dropped him, and was in the doghouse.

It happened on the side of a busy road. Jack was in his pushchair. At five months he still wasn't able to sit up by himself so I'd only loosely strapped him in. But as I tilted the front wheels down off the kerb ready to cross over, he picked that precise moment to sit up for the very first time in his life. The result was spectacular. He cantilevered over his strap, performed a perfect parabola, and finished with a beautiful swallow dive. Had Jack had something soft to land on and someone been pointing a camcorder at him, it would have been a comedy exit worthy of *You've Been Framed*. But there was nothing funny about the crunching thud as his forehead bounced off the kerbstone.

The front of the human skull is the thickest part and Jack hadn't actually fallen all that far, so the damage was superficial. Babies are surprisingly tough. One of the first stories I ever covered was about an infant who fell four storeys from a tower block and survived with nothing worse than heavy bruising.

But I was consumed with guilt, especially next morning when Jack greeted me from his cot with a gummy smile, a black eye, and an egg-shaped bump square in the centre of his forehead. There were one or two suspicious glances down at the hotel pool later.

Judy was forgiving enough – 'it could have happened when I was pushing him; stop beating yourself up' – but I knew I had let my son down. I should have strapped him in properly. What if he'd fallen into the path of a car? I shuddered.

That night we got back to our rooms after dinner at a restaurant in the next village. As I switched the car ignition off, there was a simultaneous power cut all along the coast. We laughed at the coincidence. Not for long.

'You go ahead with the boys and light candles. I'll get Jack into the carrycot and follow on.'

'OK.'

The others disappeared into the dark while I transferred Jack from his baby seat into the high-sided carrycot, and tucked him tightly in. No more cock-ups on my watch.

The sirocco was blowing, probably the reason for the electricity outage; a tree must have fallen on to power lines somewhere. As I carried my son through the near pitch-dark, only pinpricks of candlelight beginning to appear at windows, I heard a branch crashing down ahead of me from one of the palm trees that lined the path to our rooms. Careful, now.

Suddenly, white light exploded inside my head. Yes, it was another comedy classic from *père* Madeley, clown father extraordinaire. I'd trodden on the curved end of a palm branch and the whole thing upended and smacked me hard in the face. You know, that old garden rake routine.

'Fuck! Jesus! Ow!'

In the same instant the carrycot suddenly felt horribly light as it swayed violently in my hand.

Oh, please God, not again.

There instantly followed that now-familiar crunching sound as my son's face made contact with the pavement.

A couple of minutes later I arrived in our room.

'Um, Judy, look, I, er, just –'

'We've found the candles. Looks quite pretty in here, doesn't it? Can you –'

Judy, I've dropped him again. I stood on this fucking branch in the dark. I think he's all ri–'

'*Again?* You *idiot*! Let me see . . .'

We hauled Jack into the candlelight. He gave us a cheerful grin, as far as we could tell through the blood that had only just started to stop pouring from his nose.

'You're not fit to take care of a fucking *hamster*! Get ice from the freezer. I *hate* you!'

The twins beat a tactical retreat to their room.

I'd never seen my wife so angry, before or since. Once we'd established Jack wasn't seriously hurt, she swept off to bed without a word. I spent the night on a horrible plastic sofa next to my snoring son. Penance was due.

Almost all fathers drop their kids at some time or another. But not twice in two days. We laugh about it now, but at the time I felt like the most incompetent, bungling father on the planet. When I carried my battered baby to the pool next morning, the unspoken hostility from other parents there was palpable, partly because of my hangdog, guilty air. It was a good job we weren't on network television back then. The *News of the World* would have been on our case in no time.

*

Judy must have forgiven me, because when we came back from the Canaries we got married.

The ceremony took place in Manchester's registry office on

Jackson's Row, just off Deansgate. It was very different from my first wedding, not least because my son was present, as well as my stepsons, plus a large contingent from both the happy couple's families.

But, for Judy, there were undeniable echoes of her first nuptials twelve years earlier. Because they, too, had taken place in Jackson's Row. There were at least three offices couples could get married there and when we all trooped into the one designated for us, Judy whispered to me, 'I *knew* this would happen . . . they've given us exactly the same room as David and I had last time.'

Her family realised this too – after all, most of them had been there back in 1974. It didn't really matter, but it did feel a little odd.

But once the ceremony was under way, we all forgot about it and everything went swimmingly, until the designated photographer – Judy's younger brother, Roger – moved forward to snap us signing the register.

Roger is something of a perfectionist and kept adjusting the focus and getting us to alter positions slightly. Judy loathes being photographed and after a couple of times she began to fidget. 'Surely you've got enough by now?' she asked at last.

I squeezed her waist, remembering all the photoshoots we'd endured together for publicity campaigns promoting *Granada Reports*. 'Come on, darling,' I said. 'It's not as if you haven't done this before.'

The Finnigans froze. Judy stiffened. '*What?*'

Too late, the double meaning revealed itself to me.

'Oh God, I didn't mean . . . That is to say, I was talking about –'

'Never mind. Just leave it now.'

Later, in the car on the way to our reception, I managed to explain and a somewhat mollified Judy said, 'OK, but you'd better explain to my lot when we get there. God knows what they must be thinking.'

So round the room I went. 'So, you see, when I said, "It's not as if you haven't done this before," I wasn't talking about, you know, I was meaning . . .' and so on. Judy's elder brother, Cal, told me years later that I had reminded him of a slightly desperate Basil Fawlty.

Explanations over, we got on with the celebrations. It was wonderful; I felt the purest joy. I knew I had finally found the right woman for me and, halfway through the wedding breakfast, Jack woke in his carrycot at the side of our table and pushed himself up to peer over at us. I waved at him and he gave a great big gummy grin. It seemed to me like an unambiguous thumbs-up.

*

Richard. That was what the now-toddling Jack called me once he started talking. Not Dad or Daddy – Richard. And why not? It was what Tom and Dan called me. But as time went by, an increasingly sentient Jack was clearly developing some confused ideas about fatherhood.

David had arrived to collect his sons for the weekend and Jack marched up to him. 'David, are you my daddy too?'

David looked like he'd swallowed a 50p piece and after he'd

retreated in confusion, I decided it was time for a little chat with my four-year-old son.

'Mummy's your mummy, and Tom's and Dan's as well,' I explained, sitting with him on our sunny doorstep. 'They live with Mummy and me because we all thought that was best. But David's their daddy, and I'm your daddy. Do you see?'

Jack processed the information. 'So Tom and Dan have two daddies.'

'Er . . . well, sort of. I'm what's called their stepdaddy.'

'Are you my stepdaddy too?'

'No. I'm just your daddy.'

More deep thought.

'Which are best, daddies or stepdaddies?'

Now there was a question with topspin. I paused for a moment.

'Neither, really. As long as they love their children, they're about the same.'

'Does David love me?'

I tried not to smile. 'No, although I'm sure he thinks you're a nice little boy.'

'Why doesn't he love me though?'

Christ, this was getting complicated.

'Because he's not your stepdaddy. You don't live with him, do you? You live with Mummy and Daddy. See?'

Jack nodded. 'But he still loves Tom and Dan, even though he doesn't live with them any more?'

'Exactly.' I thought that was probably enough for one day but felt obliged to ask him: 'Is there anything else you want to know?'

He nodded and looked up at me intently. Here it comes. The big one.

'Can we have McDonald's?'

*

Meanwhile our family continued to grow. Judy was pregnant again, and for the first time in her life she was expecting a girl. We were thrilled, if slightly taken aback. Sons we knew we could do. Daughters were unknown territory.

Back at St Mary's, and in the same operating theatre Jack was delivered, the baby we'd decided to call Chloe was prised into the world with the same brutally efficient force as her brothers. But there was no hint of the diplodocus or brontosaur about this baby.

'My God, she's beautiful,' Judy said, as I placed Chloe on her breast. 'I mean, really, literally beautiful. Just look at her . . . she's such a little girl . . .'

It was true. With her rosebud lips and delicately lashed eyes, Chloe looked nothing like the primordially fierce Jack had in his early weeks. Or as formidable as Ustinov's newborn daughter, come to that.

That lovely, utterly peaceful atmosphere that comes just after a baby has been born had descended. Judy and her little girl drifted off to sleep. I took some Polaroids of mother and daughter gently nuzzling each other and tiptoed out. When I got home, Jack was long in bed and Anne was sitting at the kitchen table, playing cards with her twin grandsons.

'Well, what do you think?'

Anne shook her head slowly. 'Oh, Richard – she's *lovely* . . .'

'Boys?'

'Honestly?'

'Here we go . . . Of course. Just don't tell me your sister looks like a dinosaur.'

'No . . . she looks like a kitten.'

We took a marker pen and drew some whiskers on each of Chloe's pink cheeks.

Blimey. They were right.

*

Four was plenty, Judy and I decided. As she'd had quite enough of surgery, I volunteered to drop in at the Family Planning Centre for The Snip. I opted for local anaesthetic, and it lived up to its billing: it was extremely local. Too bloody local, in fact. I didn't feel a thing when the surgeon made the pre-liminary incisions with his scalpel, but when he got to the business part of chopping and tying off the tubing deep within, I felt like I'd fallen into the hands of an especially enthusiastic Gestapo doctor.

'Sorry, old boy,' he muttered apologetically as I went into vertical lift-off from the operating table, snorting and bellowing like a castrated horse. 'Looks like you've got some scar tissue down there – old sporting injury, probably. It's blocked the anaesthetic. Can't stop now though, I'm afraid.' And he sawed on.

Judy had driven me to the clinic as vasectomees weren't allowed to drive for a day or so after. When I tottered back into the waiting room, slightly greener than its painted walls, she stared at me in alarm.

'Good God. What have they done? Cut it off?'

'It's perfectly possible. That did *not* go well. Take me home. I need a massive drink.'

She was sympathetic, up to a point. Later that evening, when I described my agony in lurid terms once too often, Judy said drily, 'Hmmm. I'm sure it was horrible but try having a baby.'

'Try having your balls slit open without anaesthetic! You can't, and I can't have a baby either!'

We glared at each other for a moment, an incipient battle of the sexes crackling in the air.

But I'd overdone it, and as I grumpily went to bed I realised my wife had never really complained about the pain following her Caesarean sections. Time to pipe down about the vasectomy.

(But it really hurt. Honestly.)

My father wouldn't have dreamed of having a vasectomy and, had he been alive, he would certainly have tried to talk me out of it. Not because I would be 'shooting blanks' – he didn't think in such crude terms – but because he would have thought it fundamentally unmanly to volunteer to be sterile.

In fact there were quite a lot of 'unmanly' things my generation were willing to do within a marriage that would have been anathema to men born in the interwar years. Going with their partners to antenatal classes, for example, or appointments with the gynaecologist.

My father would have been appalled to sit in on a consultation between his wife and her 'baby doctor', let alone an examination of any kind. Stirrups and speculums? Not today, thank you. I'll be at the office.

Being present at the actual birth was another big no-no. My dad went out and mowed the lawn while I was being delivered in the front room of his home on Dagenham Road, partly for something to do, and partly to drown out the disconcerting noises drifting from the house. It simply wasn't done for fathers to watch their children being born. The delivery room was the preserve of the midwife and, if there were problems, the doctor.

It is quite incredible how quickly these attitudes changed. Centuries of received wisdom and tradition were swept away in a handful of years. As late as the 1960s, young fathers patrolled hospital corridors, chain-smoking and swapping nervous jokes with each other, while 'the wife' had their babies out of sight and out of earshot.

Yet, by the 1970s, no self-respecting young husband could refuse to be in the delivery room, holding his partner's hand, mopping her brow and tenderly urging her to 'push'.

What happened?

In Britain, it was surely a combination of feminism and its mighty war-wagon, the National Childbirth Trust. Between them, they swept away the old shibboleths surrounding men and childbirth and dragged fathers-to-be by the scruff of the neck into the delivery room. It was a matter of taking responsibility and supporting their partners, they were told firmly. And most men found, to their surprise, that they were actually happy to go. I wouldn't have missed the experience for anything.

But does it draw modern men closer to their children, 'bond' them any closer than previous generations of fathers were to theirs?

Actually, I don't think so. My father loved me no more and no less than I love my own son. That is to say, completely.

But what about the question four-year-old Jack didn't ask me that morning in his catechism on the doorstep about step-parenting? What about the four people I helped bring up, two from the age of seven, two from birth?

*

Tom and Dan; Jack and Chloe. Did I treat my children differently from my stepchildren as all of them grew up together?

We'll start with the easy bit. I certainly treated Chloe differently from all the others. Still do, always will. I've yet to meet a father with children of both sexes who wouldn't say the same.

All one's children provoke and inspire a powerful protective reflex. It never goes away. It doesn't matter how old they become or what the specific threat to them is; the instinct to circle the wagons, saddle up and ride out at the head of the rescue posse to bring one's chicks back to safety is a constant. But the quality, the flavour, the essence of that emotion differs depending on whether we're talking about a girl or a boy; a son or a daughter. At least, in my experience it does.

The protectiveness I have always felt towards Chloe has a more tender, all-encompassing nature than the more robust, critically laced support I extend to her brothers. It's more elastic. More forgiving, I suppose.

Is that sexist? I don't really care either way, although perhaps the seeds of paternal doom lie in such seeming sentimentality. *Caveat pater*. Look at what happened to Lear. Although my Chloe has more of Cordelia about her than of Goneril or Regan. Lucky for me.

I long ago gave up trying to fight or rationalise this powerful, instinctive differential. It just is. *Vive la différence*, and all that; Chloe is a girl and I treat her more gently and indulgently on most levels than I do the boys. Go fish.

It doesn't mean I love her one scintilla more or less than the others.

So what about Tom and Dan, and Jack? What about their 'differential'? Is there one? I am always being asked if I treat my stepsons differently from my own son.

Absolutely. Of course. In the same way as I treated the twins differently from each other right from the start. They may be from the same egg but they're separate human beings.

Long before Jack was born, Judy and David, and then I, would grind our teeth at school parents (and step-parents) evenings, where teachers regularly confused Tom and Dan. One couldn't really blame the faculty – the boys looked identical – but underneath the physiological genetic cloning, they were developing into psychologically separate individuals who required different approaches to parenting, and teaching.

Today, one twin has a university degree and one doesn't; one works as a pop-video director in London, the other as a fashion designer and buyer for a multinational company, living in a city hundreds of miles from his brother.

I love these young men, my first children, completely and

equally. I always did, from our very first year together when we were drenched in Cornish sunshine and later when the twins behaved with such grave courtesy before my mother.

But have I loved them as much as Jack – my first-born, their half-brother?

I certainly came to treat him differently, in his turn.

But come – no prevarications. Which is it to be; which bond has the first call on a father's and stepfather's primal emotions? Surely the selfish gene will have to make its declaration of supremacy, now we come to it?

At this point, I am seriously tempted to yawn. Because it honestly isn't like that. It doesn't have to be a case of one versus the other and neither should it be. Otherwise, why would any natural parent ever freely and lovingly adopt the children of others?

When I see our four gathered together, laughing, arguing, teasing each other, I just see four people I adore. I feel uncomplicated happiness and affection for them all. When I try and help one of them with their problems, I don't add or subtract a little extra tender loving care depending on which one carries my DNA and which one doesn't.

When their mother and I made our wills, I didn't think of putting a little extra aside for the two children whose cells come from the Madeley gene pool. If either of us had suggested it, the other would have thought they had gone mad.

They are all our children. Equal shares for all, in love and treasure.

*

'Help! Help!'

I gritted my teeth and held on tight to my squirming, kicking, yelling son as I edged my way between tables towards the restaurant exit. Jack was five now, and if I'd had hopes he would grow up as biddable and easy-going as his brothers, those hopes had faded long ago. He could be a little sod.

'Help! Somebody help me!'

'He's just doing it for effect,' I said tersely to a group of concerned diners as I sidled past, trying to keep Jack's flying feet from kicking anyone in the head. 'Everything's under control, I assure you. Excuse me, can I just . . . thank you.'

'*Help!*'

When it came to iron wills, Jack could have given Stalin a few useful pointers. He had the unyielding determination of a world-class tyrant. Once he had decided to do something – or more usually, to not do something – nothing and no one was allowed to stand in his way.

Jack's battlefield of choice was the dining table. He regarded being asked to sit down at one as a personal and grievous affront to his amour propre and his inviolable right to self-determination.

Today's outbreak of hostilities had begun that Sunday morning with a typical opening skirmish.

'What are we doing today, Daddy?'

'We're going out for Sunday lunch.'

'*No. No.* We're not, not, *not!*'

At least you couldn't accuse Jack of ambiguity in such matters. He always made his position perfectly clear from the outset.

'Yes we are. At a lovely little pub in the country, a place called the Trough of Bowland, where –'

'*Hate* the toffobolly.'

'The Trough of Bowland. You've never been there, Jack, so you can't possibly hate it, can you?'

'Yes, yes, I *can*.'

Two hours later we were in the quaint Inn at Whitewell, trying and failing to enjoy Sunday lunch. As were most of the other diners, thanks to Jack. He was using his usual tried and trusted tactics – rhythmically kicking the table, noisily refusing to eat, and demanding, over and over: 'Want to go *home*!'

'This is awful, Richard,' Judy whispered as people at other tables looked across with increasing hostility. 'He's ruining it for everyone . . . perhaps we'd just better go.'

'No. We mustn't give in to him. Appeasement never works.'

'Oh, don't be ridiculous. This is Lancashire in 1990, not Munich 1938.'

I glared at my son, now blowing noisy bubbles through a straw and throwing ice from his Coke at his sister opposite.

'Jack!'

He glared back. 'Want to *go*!'

'Right, that's it, mister. You're going all right. I'm taking you out to the car. You can sit in there while we have our lunch in peace.'

Shoulders at nearby tables sagged with relief.

Exile was our ultimate sanction and Jack hated it. Deprived of his audience he would usually subside after a few minutes and be brought back to the table, docile enough. He'd knew he'd lost a battle but not the war, and there would be other campaigns to fight.

But he never went without a struggle. Today, as I picked him up and put him over my shoulder, he called dramatically: 'No! Not the car!'

Faces turned. One or two looked slightly concerned. What was that man about to do to his little boy?

Jack's radar was good. He picked up the signals and exploited them straight away, stretching out his hands beseechingly to the room behind me.

'Not the car,' he sobbed piteously. 'Not the car, Daddy!'

There were stirrings among the tables. 'Is everything . . . all right?' a woman asked as we passed. Before I could answer the little swine on my back consolidated his grasp on the initiative.

'Help! Please help! Not the car . . . *help*!'

They must have thought I was going to lash him to one of the wheels.

'It's all right, everyone,' I said with forced cheeriness. 'Situation completely under control. He's just playing to the gallery.' Once again, I sounded like Basil Fawlty, Judy told me later.

Was that a smile of secret triumph lurking on my son's face as I strapped him into his car seat, and left him for a few minutes while I had a cigarette? It certainly looked like one. But when I returned he appeared contrite.

'Sorry, Daddy.'

'All right. Promise to be good now?'

'Promise.'

Hmm. That's what Napoleon said after his first great defeat and exile. He was already planning his comeback at Waterloo.

God knows how my father would have fought a Battle of Bowland if I'd made such a scene back then. Mealtime discipline was so much stricter in the 1960s that I can't in all honesty conceive of anything like it happening when I was a boy. Going out for meals was a rare treat, usually confined to birthdays, or on holiday where the atmosphere in the hotel dining room was almost churchlike, with everyone talking incredibly quietly, like priests in the confessional.

Nor can I imagine my parents taking me out for a meal when I was little. Restaurants were for grown-ups and older children, not tinies. They wouldn't be able to appreciate the experience.

Perhaps they were right.

Meanwhile, we didn't need a child psychologist to work out what was driving Jack's determination to call the shots at the dinner table. There were two fundamental reasons, aside from that iron will of his.

His brothers. The twins were ten years older than Jack and the poor kid was stuck in a never-ending game of catch-up with them. He yearned to have their freedoms, to be given a golden pass that would allow him access to all areas of their comparatively privileged lives. It must have been deeply frustrating for him to have to bob along so far behind in their wake.

His sister. Chloe had arrived when Jack was only thirteen months old. He was simply too young to understand what was going on, other than to instinctively grasp the primary point: that his position had been usurped. There was a new baby demanding his parents' attention, and why should he do anything but resent it? The day after Chloe was born I took Jack in to St Mary's to see his mother and meet his new sister. I'd tried to tell him what was happening but when they're barely one year old you might as well try to explain how Parliament works.

We arrived in Judy's room, where she was feeding the baby. Jack looked astonished. When I lowered him on to the bed, he kicked out at them with his foot and started to cry.

A textbook case of sibling rivalry.

Jack, then, was a completely different kettle of fish from his brothers: stroppier, angrier, endlessly assertive. Where Tom and Dan were content to negotiate with the world, Jack was more likely to chuck down the gauntlet and challenge it to a fight.

Lots of little boys are like that, I realised, but the twins had given me an easy ride by comparison and a lot of what I'd learned about the business of fatherhood with them wasn't going to work with the little box of fireworks we called Jakie-Pops; always fizzing over and popping off.

My own childhood experiences with my father didn't really help either. The dynamics of my family were so different to his – it was only me and my sister, and my mother stayed at home to look after us – that I had nothing to draw on.

I had rather more to do with bringing up Jack than his mother in the first couple of years after Chloe was born. Judy was necessarily occupied with the baby, and then succumbed to a vicious bout of post-natal depression which caused her to quietly withdraw into herself for many months, until we realised what was happening to her and sought help.

Trying to work out what made my little fireball of a boy work was a challenge. The key, I slowly discovered, was to roll with the punches as much as possible. He wasn't particularly badly behaved; he was simply trying to carve out his own niche in our complicated little family. Although his endless declarations of independence could be draining, it was usually wise to let his little storms blow themselves out. And I also learned that, with Jack, forewarned was defused. He hated surprises or suddenly announced plans. So if on Saturday I casually announced we were all going out for lunch the following day, the scale of his opposition was muted; it didn't interfere with his immediate plans and, anyway, tomorrow was another day. He'd still be grumpy at table, granted, but his full-scale guerrilla campaigns of disruption became things of the past.

Anyway, if they returned there was always The Car.

*

In the summer of 1996 we moved to London, with the transfer of our morning show from Liverpool to the capital.

I had left London twenty summers before, bouncing like a pinball between the cities of the north – Carlisle, Leeds, Manchester. Now I'd ended up back where I'd started, although in a very different neighbourhood.

Romford and the East End lay on the other side of town. The money two successful TV careers had provided bought us a large house up on one of London's ancient hills, in heavily wooded Hampstead. Not a 'mansion' as some newspapers claimed, but a comfortable family home nevertheless.

It stood facing a scrap of preserved medieval fields, the remnant of what used to be Wyldes Farm. Constable, Turner and Gainsborough once lodged at the farmhouse – which still stands – to paint in the clear country air high above toxic London, escaping its stench and smoke and disease. Now the surviving meadows, hedgerows and trees were part of a turn-of-the-century addition to the more famous heath, the Heath Extension.

It felt safe there; as safe as Old Broadway had. Families walking dogs and throwing Frisbees roamed the fields opposite. We thought it a perfect place to bring up our children, and after a long interval I again had my little make-believe corner of countryside to look at. I woke up the morning after we'd moved in, and felt like a pigeon back in its loft.

The twins had stayed behind in Manchester to begin their degree courses, but came down for our first Christmas in London.

On Christmas Day afternoon I left Judy and nine-year-old Chloe in the kitchen and wandered into the television room where Tom and Dan were watching Rory Bremner's alternative Queen's speech. Jack poked his head round the door, holding his main present, a remote-control car.

'Can I take this on to the heath? I want to see how far it goes before the signal packs in.'

I glanced through our front window. There were plenty of Christmas Day walkers out on the frosty meadow opposite.

'Sure. But stay in sight of the house and don't be too long – we'll be eating soon.'

'OK, Dad.'

And he was gone.

Tom and Dan were sitting on a sofa next to the window that looked out on to the heath. 'Just keep an eye on Jack, would you?' I asked them.

'Sure.'

They turned round every now and then to check on their ten-year-old brother.

After a few minutes, Tom stood up and peered out for a little longer.

'Has Jack come back in?' he asked me over his shoulder. 'Only I can't see him any more.'

I came over to the window. The field was much emptier now; only a few figures moved against a background of skeletal trees and an already darkening midwinter sky. Jack must have come back. I went through to the kitchen where Judy and Chloe were peering at the gravy. 'It needs more stock, Mum.'

'D'you think so? I don't want it too watery . . .'

'Has Jack come in?'

They looked vaguely at me and shook their heads. 'Don't think so.'

I went to the front door and opened it. Now the heath was completely deserted, and a little mist had begun to rise from a stream running under a hedgerow on the far side. I cupped my hands to my mouth.

'Jack!'

My voice echoed back to me, but that was the only reply. I went to the bottom of the stairs and called up to his bedroom.

'Jack! Are you up there?'

Nothing. A faint sensation of unease moved deep inside and I went back to the kitchen.

'I can't find Jack.'

Judy nodded to the back door. 'He's probably in the garden.'

'You would have seen him come through though, wouldn't you?'

She shrugged and I went to open the door. It was locked, top and bottom.

I took a deep breath and turned round.

'Seriously, Judy, he's vanished. He's not in the house, or the garden, or on the heath.'

'He must be. You can't have looked properly, that's all.'

I went back to the open front door and stared out again. It was darker now, and there was nothing moving out there.

'*Jack!*'

I crossed the road and went on to the grass. I heard voices and suddenly a couple walking their dog materialised out of some bushes. I jogged over to them.

'Have you seen a boy in a blue jumper? He'll have been playing with a remote-control car . . . a red one.'

They shook their heads. 'No, sorry . . . have you lost him?'

'I don't know . . . I mean, no. He was –'

'Is he there?' Judy called from our front steps. For the first time she sounded worried.

'No.'

The couple walked quickly on, not wanting to get involved.

By now Tom and Dan were making a room-by-room search of the house, in case Jack was playing some stupid trick, or listening to his Walkman, deaf to our calls.

I suddenly remembered the side gate to the back garden and cursed. Of course, he could have gone through that way. But when I raced on to our lawn, it was as silent and deserted as the heath opposite.

I rejoined Judy on our front steps as the twins clattered breathlessly down the stairs.

'Not there.'

'Not there.'

Judy turned to me, white and wide-eyed.

She said it first. What we'd both started thinking, at the edges of our minds.

'We've lost him. Some bastard must have seen him playing with his truck and gone over and said to him, "Hey – I've got one of those in my car. Come and have a look." Oh God, Richard, he's been taken, he's been taken.'

I looked wildly around me. We'd warned our children time without number not to go off with strangers, but it happens. A couple of years before Jack had been on his bike in Old Broadway and had ridden straight into a car cruising slowly down the street. He wasn't hurt and we were in the house, oblivious. A few minutes later he ran in to tell us what had happened and finished with the words, 'But I did cry a bit and the lady sitting next to the man driving put me on her knee and cuddled me. She was very kind, Mummy.'

I'd had visions of a latter-day Hindley and Brady on the prowl and exploded. 'You never, *ever* get into a strange car. Not *ever*!'

Now it looked like he had, and this time the Big Bad Wolf really was behind the wheel. I had a sudden, vivid image of my son panicking in some paedophile's car, now miles away somewhere on the North Circular. I pushed it away.

'Hang on. Let's think. Is there anywhere he could have gone? What about Ronnie and Jan?'

They used to live in our house. They had only moved a few hundred yards up the road, and had sons around Jack's age.

They'd become friends. Jack always asked us if he wanted to call on them but perhaps, in all the excitement of Christmas Day, he'd forgotten. I grabbed my mobile phone and punched in their number. Jan answered.

'Oh hi, Richard – Merry Christmas!'

I could hear party noises in the background, and the squeal of children's voices.

'Jan, is Jack there?'

My voice had cracked slightly, and she sounded startled as she said quickly, 'Why? What's wrong?'

'Is he there?'

'I don't think so. But the house is full of kids. Hold on, I'll check.'

She left the receiver swaying on the end of its flex and I heard it bumping lazily against the wall. Time seemed to slow and settle along with the swinging phone. Then it snapped back into gear as the receiver rattled. Jan was back on the line.

'No, he's definitely not here – he hasn't been round for a couple of days. Is everything OK?'

That was that, then. The last door behind which our son might have been standing had slammed shut. Game over. Try again.

I stared at my wife. 'I'm calling the police.'

She nodded hopelessly and sagged against the doorframe.

Dialling 999 seemed like the end of all hope; an abject admission that we'd failed to keep our child safe; surrendered him to the beasts of the forest. As I pressed the second nine I could see Tom and Dan darting about in the dusk on the heath, looking into bushes and ditches.

Every parent's worst nightmare was taking solid form in front of us.

As I was about to complete the triple sequence, I suddenly remembered one last door we hadn't tried. Our neighbours, an American couple, had a dog, a big grey Weimaraner called Sophie. Sometimes Jack went round to play with her. He always checked with us first, but . . .

I walked up their front path, praying fiercely. 'God, let him be here. If you don't, we've lost him. Make him be here. If you don't, we've lost him. Let him be here.'

A couple passing by on the pavement heard me muttering to myself and stared for a moment before hurrying on.

I pressed the doorbell but couldn't hear anything. It didn't seem to be working, so I hammered on the door with my fist.

'Is he there?' Judy called from our front step.

'Hold on.' I banged on the door again, but there was no answer. Fuck, fuck, fuck, they were out. I turned away in despair, reaching for my phone again, but suddenly heard the faint sound of voices as a distant door opened. The family were at the back of the house, in their big kitchen. Footsteps approached and a lock and chain rattled.

The front door swung open and a blast of warmth and smell of cooking hit me. Our neighbour, Sandy, cracker hat askew and glass of wine in hand, swayed slightly before me. 'Hey, Richard! Merry Christmas!'

'Is Jack here?'

She blinked in surprise. Oh, God . . .

'Sure, didn't you know? He's out back with Sophie getting

her to chase his new truck. We were just going to . . .' She stared at me. 'Richard . . . are you OK?'

My legs had given way and I was breathing oddly.

'We've been . . . we couldn't find him, Sandy. He was on the heath and then . . . he wasn't. We looked everywhere. We thought he'd been . . .'

Her eyes widened.

'Oh my God, I'm so sorry, we thought you knew he was here . . . I'm so sorry.'

Sophie came rushing out barking furiously, Jack on her heels.

'Hi, Dad. Is our Christmas dinner ready? They've nearly finished theirs here . . .'

When I'd been Jack's age there was a big fire at the gasworks at the end of Crow Lane. My mates and I watched, thrilled, as the fierce jet of flame thundered from a ruptured pipe directly on to one of the gasometers, blistering the paint and turning the metal beneath it a dull red. We'd managed to sneak through the police cordon and were up nice and close to the action. Then we were spotted, bundled into a squad car and driven home.

My mother's language, when the officers on the doorstep explained what her son had been up to, was unprecedented.

Thirty years later, on another doorstep, history repeated itself.

Word for word.

*

I will never forget the animal intensity of my emotions over that thirty minutes on a Christmas Day; the relentless acceleration of dread and fear, culminating in the absolute certainty that my son had been abducted. Even now my heart trembles at the memory of it, and yet all was well, nothing was wrong; happy endings all round. But what a glimpse into darkness those minutes provided; a very facsimile of hell.

Later, the children in bed, I reached for my Shakespeare and searched for Macduff's haunting, horrified words when told that his children have been murdered.

'Did you say all . . . all? What! All my pretty chickens . . .?'

I shivered and put the book back.

I said happy endings all round – not quite. The flash of completely unreasonable anger I felt towards my son when I found him at last was almost as fierce as the panic that preceded it, and it took a while to fade. Perhaps, too, there was a faint echo of my father's propensity to explode with rage. I don't know. But I assumed at the time this was a one-way passage of emotion; a strictly father-to-son, adult-to-child reaction. But a few years later I discovered this was wrong, and that the channel of relief and recrimination after a great scare flows just as strongly in the reverse direction.

We were celebrating my niece's eighteenth birthday at a restaurant called the Blue Strawberry. In hindsight its strange name carried a hint of warning.

Our sprawling family party had commandeered a huge table and, as is usual when we all gather together, the conversational volume control was set to eleven. I was having a fierce argument with my sister's husband about the current television remake of *The Forsyte Saga*. The nation was split over the casting of Gina McKee as Irene, originally played by the fragrant

Nyree Dawn Porter. I was with the half who thought McKee was terrific; my brother-in-law, Peter, was scathing.

He'd just made rather a good point and I intended to counter it. So I swallowed the entire chunk of rare beef I'd just forked into my mouth, wanting to return to the fray without delay.

I opened my mouth, but no words came. The slick piece of meat had wrapped itself snugly across the top of my windpipe, and I couldn't make a sound. Neither could I breathe.

Choking – proper choking, I mean, not the coughing and spluttering we all make when something goes down the wrong way (if you can cough and splutter you're OK) – is the most extraordinarily sinister physical experience I have ever had. I must have exhaled just before swallowing so I had very little air in my lungs; no reservoir of oxygen to compress upwards to punch out the obstruction. I sat in complete silence, trying to work out what to do. My brother-in-law thought I'd been silenced by his rapier thrust and turned to talk to someone else.

In the middle of this raucous family gathering, I was instantaneously trapped in my own little world.

I wrapped my arms around myself and tried to squeeze my ribcage in a sort of self-delivered bear hug. No dice. Then I thrust hard backwards into my chair and strained every muscle to try and deliver a cough. Not even the tiniest hack. My chest was locked in paralysis.

By now I'd started to drool slightly and black spots were beginning to appear in front of my eyes. Uh-oh.

Still no one noticed anything was wrong, even though I hadn't spoken for at least thirty seconds (unheard of). I pushed my chair back with a crash and stood up, bending low over the table and hammering it as hard as I could with my fists, not to attract attention but in an instinctive attempt to dislodge the blockage. It didn't work but people now looked across at me curiously.

'What on earth's he doing?'

My face was beginning to turn as blue as the proverbial strawberry and Peter suddenly shouted, 'Christ – he's choking!'

Uproar. Fists crashing on my back (Judy's). Bigger fists (Pete's). Still the fucking thing in my throat wouldn't budge, and now the dark spots were multiplying into a grey blizzard.

Strangely, the initial panic that had swept through me now faded, and I was able to think perfectly clearly. I remember telling myself: 'This is a stupid way to die' and a very high whine began droning in my head, exactly like a mosquito hovering over one's ear on a hot summer night.

Still the pounding behind me went on, and still my respiratory system was stuck in stubborn lockdown.

Then I heard a new noise, not from inside my head but from the rapidly shrinking world in front of me as my peripheral vision shorted out. It was the sound of glasses and bottles being scattered as my sister, on the far side of the room, leaped on to the table and strode across it yelling 'Get out of the way!' with all the authority of the teacher that she is.

Elizabeth jumped down behind me and wrapped her arms around my lower chest, making a hard fist just below the sternum. Ah, I thought almost lazily, the old Heimlich manoeuvre. Good for sis.

Doctors say if you find yourself having to administer the Heimlich manoeuvre, you shouldn't be afraid to break a few ribs in the process, and my big sister certainly wasn't. The violent squeeze she delivered made all those thumps on my back feel like kindly pats.

But it didn't work. Not in the slightest degree. She tried again, and again, but my trachea stubbornly refused to release its grip on the intruder it had decided was trying to infiltrate the lungs beneath.

It's called the drowning reflex. A sphincter muscle at the top of the windpipe instantly seals the tube shut when water tries to get in. If you're drowning it's the body's way of buying a little extra time for you to get to the surface or be rescued, because the moment you inhale water, you're pretty much finished. But the trachea can't tell the difference between drowning and choking, and the conscious brain can't override the primitive reflex that's been triggered deep in the cerebral cortex. This evolutionary conundrum was now in the process of efficiently killing me, albeit in a companionable silence. Our little secret, which the way things were going it looked like I was about to carry with me to the grave.

Liz had started to panic. From what seemed like a great distance I heard her screaming, 'Help! Somebody help me!' I remembered Jack's performance in another restaurant a long time ago, and smiled inwardly. I was quite calm now, and resigned. Another final coping reflex, apparently. A little home-brewed morphine to ease the crossing.

I managed to lift my head slightly as the light finally began to fade away altogether, and saw my daughter weeping hysterically on the far side of the table, her face pressed into her hands. I couldn't see Judy – she was behind me – but Jack was turned to the wall, beating it with both palms. I felt terribly sorry for all of them, having to see this awful finale; but was perfectly relaxed nevertheless. It was just time to go, that was all.

Perhaps it was my legs finally giving way that did it. As I buckled towards the floor my sister gave another despairing squeeze, the strongest yet, as if to drag me back. Muscle power combined with gravity and the rock in my throat moved for the first time since I'd swallowed it nearly three minutes before. It lifted very slightly, like a hinged lid on a bottle, and I managed to gulp in a tiny gasp of air before my stupid suicidal windpipe jealously grabbed the lump back again.

Liz felt it. 'I think it's coming!' She gave another vicious heave.

Now I had a little air to work with I managed a tiny cough at the same time and up shot the vile – and by now almost liquid – piece of meat, into my mouth. I spat it out with what looked like contempt but was pure relief, and sucked in the biggest lungful of air in my entire life. Sound and vision flickered for a moment, and then snapped back to normal. All systems go.

Laughter. Tears. Cheers. I hugged my sister, I hugged my wife, I hugged my sister again. Chloe was suddenly in my arms too.

'Oh, Daddy, I thought you were dying . . .'

'I can assure you I was, chicken,' I croaked, 'but it's all right now . . . I'm fine now.'

Then Jack appeared in front of me, cheeks wet with tears, hair wild, face contorted with fury. He pointed a trembling finger right into my face.

'*Never. Eat. Again.*'

There was a moment's pause and then everyone except Jack cracked up. He looked round in angry confusion.

'I mean, never eat *meat* again . . . I'm serious, Dad. Don't ever do that again . . . please . . .' And he burst into tears.

He was easily the most affected person in the room. Jack was sixteen when his Pa nearly expired before his very eyes, but even now, in his twenties, he looks up in alarm if I so much as clear my throat while I'm eating. His anger with me that day was an interesting reflection of my own with him the Christmas he went missing. Perhaps men instinctively resent having their deepest emotions disturbed unnecessarily as things turn out; an atavistic sense that their feelings have been toyed with needlessly.

Judy certainly wasn't angry with Jack when I discovered him next door that Christmas Day. She was just suffused with relief. Meanwhile, within minutes of my sister saving my life, both Elizabeth and Judy were making dry jokes at my expense about what had just happened. Even Chloe started teasing me before we'd even left the restaurant.

Jack, though, sat in brooding silence. Even today, I don't think he has quite forgiven me. Whenever the subject comes up, his face sets and he becomes monosyllabic before, usually, leaving the room. I frightened him that day, badly, and he's still not quite over it. Come to think of it, neither am I. I tend to steer clear of roast beef now.

*

After my father died I occasionally dreamed he'd survived his heart attack and was recovered. I always woke angrily from these dreams. In the moments that they still held sway over my consciousness I felt he'd somehow tricked us all, and me in particular, with a cruel joke that he had no business playing on any of us.

Then I'd remember, and the return of reality was almost a comfort, if a cold one. All that pain and grief hadn't been for nothing, then.

My sister had such dreams too, but she took succour from them.

Strange, that difference.

Considering it now, I think the primal male anger which sometimes runs parallel with other emotions exchanged between fathers and sons tells us something. Their connections are hard-wired in a quite different way to the relationship between fathers and their daughters, or mothers and their children.

Some of these inter-male emotions and responses are non-negotiable; as specific and almost as physical as a mother's response to her baby's hunger cries, stimulating a reflex to produce milk. But how are the connections between fathers and their sons formed? Which ones are intrinsic to the relationship, and which are created by events, past and present?

Now, as my son moves into his adulthood, I feel as if I stand on one of the great fault lines of my life, an elevated ridge between tectonic plates. Ahead lies the future; mostly a smooth, featureless land. But when I turn around I look across a continent sculpted and scarred by the unalterable past.

From here I can see the road that winds through a century of my paternal family history. Jack and I stand in the foreground.

Behind us, in the middle distance, is Christopher, and further away, looking sadly at his son, Geoffrey. Distant but discernible, Henry stands, frozen in his moment of decision more than one hundred years ago. A choice he could neither revise nor revisit.

Henry's abandonment of his son at Kiln Farm conferred an icy childhood on the boy. In turn, a glacier ground its way inexorably into my father's life.

Perhaps Geoffrey could have tried harder to block or divert the freezing flow, but fate – and Uncle William – conspired against him.

When my father arrived in Canada he found a way to escape the cold past. That was thanks to my mother and the warmth of her family life there. Emotionally defrosted, Christopher did everything he could to reinvent himself and become a loving father to his children.

He wasn't entirely successful. The suppressed rage that found an outlet in my beatings took a long time to subside. And my father never regained the self-belief that had been extinguished by his father's lack of affection.

But he did enough. He did enough. His children grew up secure in their father's love, and that was a huge achievement, a true reversal of fortune.

I have often wondered how the consequences that flowed from the fateful decision made by 'Bulford from Birmingham' so long ago may have rippled into my life and influenced my behaviour as a father.

Fragments of the past, certainly, have washed up on my shores. But I think that, mostly, they are reactive agents.

For example, my father lacked self-confidence; as a

consequence I have too much of it. That can be dangerous (and overconfidence is not an attractive quality, either). I am certain it was at the root of my catastrophic oversight at a supermarket checkout when I was in my early thirties. I forgot to pay for a stack of items in the front section of my trolley, because my mind was in overdrive planning the rest of a busy busy day. I thought I could handle everything and anything and forgot that the devil lurks in the detail. What a demon sprang out of my oversight! I ended up having to argue my innocence before a judge and jury.

As I have become older, I have had to fashion tools to hack away at the hubris to which I am prone. My marriage has helped me do this; Judy is inclined to pessimism and this has acted as a gentle but constant counterweight to my sometimes overweening optimism.

I loathe corporal punishment, for what I think are obvious reasons. But would I have done so if it wasn't so morally unfashionable (not to say illegal) today? After all, my father was soundly beaten as a child both at home and at school and those experiences didn't deter him from enthusiastically taking a cane to me.

But whatever the modish circumstances, I think I would have always hated the idea of visiting such cruelty on my son. Just as Christopher swore to himself that he would show his children love in a way that his father could not, I promised myself, even when I was a boy, that I would never inflict the pain and humiliation of a thrashing on my own son.

It was probably my first genuine resolution.

But the real connective strand that binds together my father, grandfather and me only became fully clear to me during the writing of this book. It can be expressed in a mantra that I am certain never left my grandfather's lips, although he followed its dictum faithfully from the moment he was left behind in 1907. It is a creed that allowed him to be reconciled with his family in Canada two decades later.

To understand all is to forgive all.

On the very morning of Geoffrey's abandonment, William and Thomas and Sarah explained to the frantic boy standing before them the exact nature of the agreement with Henry. From that moment he had not the slightest doubt that he had been pawned by his father, and that the ticket with his name on it could only be redeemed when he was twenty-one. From the very first, he understood the fate that had befallen him and who was responsible for it. And yet he forgave them all.

He understood Henry's predicament all those years before. And he forgave him for the way he had resolved it. The alternative – to condemn his father for the betrayal, rail at his mother for her submission to it, curse his siblings for their good fortune at his expense – might have been satisfying and more than justified; but ultimately it would have been nihilistic.

Geoffrey wanted to rebuild and reconnect, not destroy.

My father, in his turn, understood the reasons his father had slowly evolved into a man who found it so difficult to demonstrate affection. He knew Geoffrey's back story well enough; he told it to me enough times, and sympathetically too. But like his father before him, he wanted to salvage what he could from a poor situation. He had no interest in playing the blame game.

The one thing he never really understood was why he'd

been packed off to Denstone, but he chose to write that riddle off and refused to take his father to task about it. Instead, he tried all his life to build bridges with Geoffrey. And he succeeded. They both succeeded in the end. They found a language through which they could, at last, communicate emotionally. Music was the salve and blessing that healed and united Geoffrey and Christopher. I know it was. I saw it with my own eyes, working on them, bringing them closer.

And me?

To understand all is to forgive all.

My father's extraordinary confessional to his young son on the road from London to Shawbury the morning after he had beaten me so recklessly and severely, was a defining moment in both our lives. I instinctively accepted the explanation for his behaviour, and trusted his sincerity when he promised me it would never be repeated.

I understood and I forgave. He never gave me cause to regret that.

And Jack?

I think it's time my son spoke for himself.

Epilogue

I never met my grandfather Christopher and so, for reasons that I'm sure are more to do with my painfully short attention span than my dad withholding information, I never knew the story of his life, or his father's.

The occasional conversation I had with Dad about Chris and Geoffrey left me with a vague awareness of my great-grandfather's abandonment, but in my mind our family history was always coloured with an atmosphere of mystery and adventure. They were merely bedtime stories, or casual but interesting and insightful anecdotes Dad would relate to me whenever we found ourselves on a day out together, or sharing a long car journey. Simply put, these were stories and nothing more, tales that I could never truly identify with because I'd never actually met either man. Both had died long before I was born.

If I'm brutally honest, up until a few years ago, I couldn't even remember my grandfather's first name. I would constantly confuse it with my mother's dad's. This other grandfather also died before I was born, and his name too had little meaning for me. In fact, if anyone were to have shown me a photo of the two men I would have had a tough time deciding who was who.

Then, one afternoon in 2001, Dad came back from his mother's house with a collection of photographs documenting his childhood, adolescence and early professional life. I remember sifting through them, smiling and cringing at the woeful 1970s progressive folk-rock haircut he sported throughout his late teens and early twenties. It was weird seeing him at the same stage of life that I was now passing through – the same awkward, lanky teenager I saw each time I looked in the mirror. These glimpses of my own father's youth – hanging out with his mates, smoking cigarettes, generally messing around – had a distinct and profound impact on me. They provided me with a strange comfort. I was a difficult teenager, and I think between the ages of fifteen and seventeen my dad and me found our relationship under strain, for the first time. As Christopher had lamented to his wife years before, there was simply 'too much testosterone in the house'.

Looking at those photos for the first time allowed me to see my dad in an entirely different light, one that was much-needed so I could understand one of the most undeniable truths of myself and my father's relationship; the fact that we are the same. However much I deny it, however much I try to ignore it, Dad and I are pretty much identical in terms of our most inherent character traits. For example, our tempers are bloody awful. Although Dad has had nearly three decades more than me to work on his inner Zen, we both needlessly get wound up by small and insignificant provocations. Our memories are also useless, something Dad has had to shore up through a much-laughed-at system within our house of writing notes for himself; notes to remind him of even the most basic task he has to perform that day.

In short, I was able to see my dad as a person, a human being as opposed to simply my father. I think this understanding was a seminal point in our relationship, and one that brought us undeniably closer.

As I glanced through those old, dusty photos, I gained my first proper understanding that my dad had . . . well, actually had his own dad. This may sound ridiculously naive, and of course I knew that my father had not been raised single-handedly by my grandma. But every third or fourth photo that I came across depicted my father with a tall, smartly dressed man with strong features, a wide grin and broad shoulders. To my eyes he looked the very model of a real-life incarnation of Clark Kent (the precise description Dad would later offer, in this book).

To see my elusive grandfather staring back at me, happy, smiling and alive, triggered a strange feeling of emotional connection. The only other time I had ever felt anything like this was when Dad took me to see his father's grave in Essex. Yet the feeling that gripped me the first time I witnessed, in the photos, my father sitting, laughing and joking with his father, was very different. I could suddenly see my dad, not as a father, but as a son. And in the strangest way, I at last saw my grandfather, Christopher, for the first time.

A sense of guilt began to build within me. I felt selfish and self-absorbed. I had never given Christopher any thought. The idea that I was part of a legacy, of sorts – that my life and upbringing was inexorably linked with such recent generations – had never even occurred to me before. Before this mild epiphany, the only part of Christopher's legacy that I recognised resided in my father's desire to keep a healthy heart. After quitting smoking nearly two decades ago, Dad became a keen cyclist and walker. This, I assumed, was down to a very natural desire to escape his own father's fate. To my mind, this was the extent of 'Grandpa's' psychological and physiological legacy to his son. As to what kind of father he had been to my own, I hadn't a clue.

Now I know. The pages preceding these have provoked a similar but much stronger reaction to the one I had years ago when I flicked through those old family photographs. The life of my great-grandfather Geoffrey – permeated with a constant feeling of loss, disappointment and abandonment – is an unimaginable world away from the comfortable, affectionate upbringing afforded to me. The bleak and harsh reality Geoffrey was confronted with at such a vulnerable age encompassed not only loss but, obviously, a deep sense of betrayal. Henry's decision was by no means an easy one, but it is hard to imagine any father now resorting to such cold, sad practicality. But this is the problem, for me. I find it hard to imagine because the relationship I have with my father is a loving one, built on a mutual feeling of trust and care. Essentially, I know that Dad will always be there for me. As I will for him. This may sound cheesy or clichéd, but it is sincere – absolute certainties that I hold very close to my heart.

I was fascinated by the sentence my father used to describe Christopher's reconciliation with his own father: 'It's never too late to salvage something from the wreckage.' Henry's 'deal' with his brother spawned deep-rooted psychological issues that I think are, even now, being confronted by my dad. In the end I found the answer to an eternal challenge; one that Dad grappled with following his father's last, terrible beating of him. *Fathers & Sons* is an exploration of the power of forgiveness and the importance of change. Geoffrey forgave Henry, Christopher forgave Geoffrey, and Dad forgave Christopher. The only difference with me is, I have nothing to forgive. It seems the dark repercussions that plagued these men who preceded me have finally been dissolved by the writing of this book.

Rather than compiling a mere documentation of a family legacy, my father has – perhaps unconsciously – succeeded in performing a kind of exorcism. The sins of the father that were visited upon Geoffrey, Christopher and Richard have quietly evaporated in the telling.

That I was spared from them is something I can't thank my own dad for enough.

JACK MADELEY, Cornwall, June 2008.

Acknowledgements

I wish to thank firstly my mother for her endless patience as I bombarded her with questions about the past. While it gave her immense pleasure to return to some of the memories, others were painful and recollection brought tears. Not only her own.

My cousin Peter was immensely helpful with factual details of our grandfather's early life and gave me an alternative family account of how Geoffrey might have been left behind at Kiln Farm in 1907. He also corrected long-held misconceptions about Sarah who, I discovered, had tried so hard to be a mother to the abandoned boy.

My literary agent, Luigi Bonomi, came up with the idea for this book after a long lunch during which we swapped our family histories. His advice during the writing of it was invaluable.

Suzanne Baboneau at Simon & Schuster gave unstinting guidance and support, as well as friendship. Her wise notes to me after I submitted the first draft of *Fathers & Sons* were a model of how to reconcile tact with frankness. Her encouragement throughout was endlessly reassuring.

Finally, my son Jack, who somehow found time to read the manuscript while taking his finals at university, and wrote the touching epilogue. I will never threaten to lock him in my car again.